"In *Bigger & Better*, Prozan outlines the principles and operating guidelines to scale a business quickly with fiscal responsibility in mind. Her thoughtful approach to building, honing, and leveraging channel partnerships can create momentum and long-term enterprise value. A definitive playbook for lean hypergrowth."

—RATHNA SHARAD, *Founder & CEO of FlavorCloud*

"This is the ultimate playbook for lean hypergrowth. Prozan's non-transactional method for profitably scaling revenue laid out in *Bigger & Better* is something I have experienced firsthand as a partner through her activation of alliances. Here, she shares her methodology that has led to significant exits by building enterprise value through relationship-based owned channels."

—CALLUM CAMPBELL, *CEO of Linnworks*

"Esther is a motivated, intelligent, and proactive partner who has spent her career shaping small, high-potential businesses into powerhouses. In *Bigger & Better*, she shares her savvy approach to scaling business leads to profitable growth while applying basic principles on building long-term success through investing in core infrastructure, people, and processes. She delivers both on partner and employee satisfaction, and she is a reliable partner I have come to know and rely on over the years."

—**BRITA TURNER FIELDING,** *US Head of Operational Strategy,* GM *of Home & Garden at eBay*

"In her book, Esther reminds us that our 'direction as a company is the accumulation of thousands of decisions' that we make as leaders every day. With *Bigger & Better*, Esther has provided a practical framework for successful decision-making. *Bigger & Better* is a must-have playbook for efficiently and profitably scaling your small business."

—**JANET MEGDADI,** VP *of Global Sales Strategy and Transformation at Visa*

"Esther has been a go-to advisor to me for quite some time now, so to get her thoughts and strategies in this format is immensely helpful. Whether you are just beginning your journey, experiencing hypergrowth, or running a large stable business, you will gain wisdom, insight, and creative strategies from this book. A particular favorite of mine is Esther's chapter on Radical Generosity—this is rarely talked about and, in my experience, pays significant dividends."

—**BEN SMITH,** COO *at Earth Breeze, former* COO *of Athletic Greens*

"In my role as CEO and President of Radial Inc., a major e-commerce logistics company, I watched Esther dramatically scale revenues profitably at Ruby Has, a company in the same space as Radial, leading to its acquisition by Shipmonk in a PE-backed deal. In *Bigger & Better*, she shares mindset principles and a lean tactical approach that leads to outsized revenue results. This is the playbook for scaling your revenues while preserving resources."

—**ILIAS SIMPSON**, *President, Modivcare and former CEO & President of Radial Inc.*

"I've witnessed firsthand Esther's remarkable approach to both business and to making the world a better place. In *Bigger & Better*, she outlines highly effective principles for disciplined business growth with limited resources by drawing from her extensive experience in driving revenue growth while maintaining high profit margins (e.g., 10X revenue growth, 1500% ARR growth in less than three years in her last role). Anyone charged with scaling revenues dramatically should make use of this playbook."

—**SANJEEV MATHUR**, *COO Kindthread, former SVP of Global Operations at Bombas*

"A must-read playbook of proven strategies and tactics for scaling with limited resources. Most small companies go out of business and never break through the barriers to survive and grow. Prozan has scaled growth dramatically on a shoestring budget and shares a practical toolkit of mindset and tactical principles so others can replicate that success."

—**VICTOR COHN**, *Chairman, Solebury Capital*

"Esther has cracked the code for how to scale revenue dramatically for companies with constrained resources while simultaneously growing ARR and EBITDA. Her mindset and tactical principles build a strong, repeatable methodology that founders and their growth teams can apply to their own growth strategies—regardless of industry or geography."

—**DAPHNE CARMELI**, *former VP at Target,*
Founder & CEO of Deliv, 9 Exits

"The definitive how-to for small businesses seeking to thrive in their sector and succeed where so many others have failed. Whether you're thinking of starting a small business or already have, with *Bigger & Better*, Esther takes her experience in scaling over 10x in three years with a minimal budget and challenges you to think strategically, listen, adapt, and give more than you take. The ultimate tool kit for small business owners."

—**NAOMI GONZALEZ**, *Co-Founder of TomboyX*

"This book is the perfect antidote to the hamster wheel of chaotic startups clinging largely or solely to paid digital marketing tactics to acquire new customers without a vision. It is a smart tactical guide to growing your business while providing lasting value to your customers. Esther takes a strategic view, shifting mindsets while sharing results-driven methodologies to get to meaningful growth. Every business should take a page out of this playbook!"

—SIOBHÁN LONERGAN, *Chief Brand Officer, SimpleHealth, Shapermint, and Thinx*

"Esther's book, *Bigger & Better*, is an ultimate guide for a startup or a growing team to scale up! It is loaded with principles, strategies, and fresh perspectives that many business owners will learn a lot from. Definitely a gem and should be on every entrepreneurs'entrepreneur's reading list."

—CHAD RUBIN, *Founder of Profasee, Co-Founder of Skubana*

"I have worked with Esther extensively and directly experienced her unique approach to scaling businesses quickly when resources are limited. As a previous founder, I found this book a must-read if you have a startup or any small company and want to grow fast. She has become a consummate authority on this topic, and *Bigger & Better* shares what is hands-down the best playbook for growth within the constraints we all have."

—JESÚS SÁNCHEZ, *Head of Industry,*
E-commerce, and Retail at Google

"Prozan is a wonderful example of someone who has a proven history of scaling small companies into great enterprises. Prozan has always been a firm believer in the importance of scaling revenue efficiently and has established herself as a mentor and dedicated speaker in the field. *Bigger & Better*...should be at the top of anyone's reference list when looking to scale a company."

—*INC. MAGAZINE*

Bigger & Better

A PLAYBOOK FOR QUICKLY
SCALING YOUR SMALL COMPANY
WITH LIMITED RESOURCES

Esther Kestenbaum Prozan

WINDERMERE
PRESS

BIGGER & BETTER
A Playbook for Quickly Scaling Your Small
Company with Limited Resoures
First Edition

ISBN   978-1-962341-07-3   *Hardcover*
       978-1-962341-06-6   *Paperback*
       978-1-962341-08-0   *Ebook*

For my sons, Itamar, Yakov, Aharon, and Netanel,
and for my bonus children, Noah and Nicole:
I love you to the moon and back.

"So David triumphed over the Philistine with a sling and a stone; without a sword in his hand."

—1 SAMUEL 17:50

Contents

Preface

RECENT CAUTIONARY TALES

In light of the principles that are discussed in this book (and that I've observed in the working world), there have been some cautionary tales very recently that bear mentioning at the outset. Of course, we're all familiar with the tale of Adam Neumann and WeWork, the so-called "billion dollar loser", which has inspired books, countless articles, and even an Apple TV+ miniseries starring Jared Leto and Anne Hathaway.

The company, which provides co-workspaces for tech start-ups, rose to tremendous prominence in the years after the Great Recession. Neumann, the company's founder, managed to amass billions of dollars in venture capital, but he lacked a self-sustaining business model or operational discipline.

In 2019, when WeWork filed an initial public offering (IPO), the company's mismanagement and unusual behavior was exposed to public ridicule. It was revealed that, despite bringing in a ton of investor money, WeWork was actually burning through cash at an alarming rate. As a result of these revelations, the IPO failed, and the company's valuation tanked by 70 percent. Neumann was offered a $1.7 billion package by the company's largest investor, SoftBank, if he would agree to leave the company entirely.[1]

Sadly, the WeWork story is not unique. At the time of this writing, we're seeing a kind of tectonic shift in the market, and a number of high-profile companies have recently gone through arcs that echo the WeWork story in a variety of ways. At the same time, the market has taken a downturn, inflation is on the rise, and businesses are being impacted by rising interest rates.

At a minimum, this is a market correction, and depending on how you look at it, we may be approaching levels that indicate a coming recession. Over the past few weeks, we have seen companies including Microsoft, Facebook, Salesforce, and Amazon lay off tens of thousands of employees, with most of them citing that they overspent on head count. By the time you read this, the picture

---

1   Deeptesh Sen, "WeCrashed: What Really Happened to WeWork?" *Indian Express*, March 19, 2022, https://indianexpress.com/article/explained/wecrashed-what-happened-to-wework-7826500/.

will probably be much clearer. However, the concept of managing a business to rigorous fundamentals has become more important than ever. Even in Silicon Valley, where the idea of "burning money to make money" was born, we're seeing a greater focus on the fundamentals and unit economics.

In this climate, some recent business stories that mirror the WeWork debacle serve as cautionary tales. Consider the chilling example of Fast, a checkout technology company. Fast managed to raise $120 million. The lead investor was Stripe, a giant publicly traded fintech company, and the ethos behind the investment was very much that Silicon Valley mindset.[2]

Fast spent money wildly. According to an article in the tech-publication *The Information*, they swiftly hired hundreds of employees, including some highly paid executives. Indeed, as one anonymous former employee put it, "With Fast, it was like, 'How quickly can we set money on fire?'"[3]

Within about a year, Fast had burned through all of their money, while only generating $600,000 in revenue (not profit, but

2   Bobby Allyn, "Fast, the Checkout Startup, Shuts Down after Burning Investors' Money," NPR, April 5, 2022, https://www.npr.org/2022/04/05/1091077398/checkout-startup-fast-is-shutting-down-after-burning-through-investors-money.

3   Kate Clark, "Fast, a Startup Backed by Stripe, Discusses Billion-Dollar Valuation," *The Information*, November 2, 2022, https://www.theinformation.com/articles/fast-a-startup-backed-by-stripe-discusses-billion-dollar-valuation.

revenue!). Much of their investment money was dumped into deals that were intended to create marketing buzz (e.g., partnering with professional sports teams).

When they ran out of money, Fast tried to raise more. They had a mindset like a lot of the startups that said, "Investors will always put more money in because they want to protect the money they've *already* put in." Indeed, founders will often make a "cash call" to their original investors and say something like, "Here's what we've done so far. Now, we need more money so we can take the next step." And it usually works, unless things are going abysmally.

However, Fast couldn't find anyone willing to invest more money, even in a down round. In a down round, investors put in money at a lower valuation than before; but Fast couldn't raise any money at all, no matter how compromising the valuation. As a result, in a turn of events that felt unprecedented in the recent memory of Silicon Valley, the company suddenly shut its doors.

Often, a company that is forced to shut down can at least sell their assets to recover some of the money. *Someone* will buy the technology and keep the product alive in some form or fashion. However, in this case, no one wanted anything from Fast. People who visited the website were confronted with a shocking and unexpected sight.

Buyer Community,

After making great strides on our mission of making buying and selling frictionless for everyone, we have made the difficult decision to close our doors. With that, we regret to share that we will discontinue Fast Checkout as a payment method for you to use on your favorite sellers.

I will be forever grateful to customers all over the world who loved using Fast to shop at their favorite brands. You shared our vision for improving the customer experience for online shopping and we can't thank you enough for putting your trust in us.

While you'll no longer use the Fast button at checkout, we are incredibly proud of the team we assembled and our work to democratize commerce through Fast's one-click checkout experience. Sometimes trailblazers don't make it all the way to the mountain top. But even in those situations, they pave a way that all others will follow. Fast has done that with bringing one-click and headless checkout into the mainstream. Buying online has been forever changed by the incredible team at Fast. The dedication, brilliance and spirit of this remarkable team is unparalleled and will forever be the legacy of Fast.

We will permanently discontinue service of Fast Checkout on April 15, 2022

With gratitude—Domm Holland

This is the equivalent of turning up to the exciting new shop in your neighborhood on a Monday morning and finding a "Permanently Closed" sign in the window—but in this case, because it was a B2B technology company, many of their customers' businesses were left in the lurch. In the end, Fast proved to be a tremendous cautionary tale.

Then there was Bolt, another company in the checkout technology space, which dramatically raised $1.3 billion. That's a crazy amount of money, but Bolt proved to be a house of cards. As it turned out, Bolt was able to raise the money at each stage using a number of data points that weren't exactly true. They also managed to partner with Authentic Brands Group, a well-known e-commerce and retail conglomerate, based on promises that were never realized.

Bolt sold call warrants to Authentic Brands Group, which gave Authentic Brands the ability to buy shares in Bolt at a later date in a preferred manner. In return, they promised to deliver fintech to associated brands by a certain date that would enable them to fast-forward their growth.

Ultimately, the technology was not delivered at a functional level, and Bolt ran out of money. At the time of this writing, Authentic Brands is suing Bolt for not fulfilling their promise. Even with the insane amount of money that Bolt raised, they were still unable to build the technology. They leveraged the fact that they'd signed with Authentic Brands in order to raise the rest of their money, but they never actually delivered a product that worked.

By signing with Authentic Brands, they essentially bought their own customers, which gave them a certain appearance of success. They used their customers' good name in place of their own merit and leveraged it heavily to sign additional deals. But it was practically a Ponzi scheme, because they fulfilled none of the deals they signed, even as they continued signing them.

We're seeing these kinds of cautionary tales crop up more frequently in our current economic environment. Even companies that operate at a high standard of accountability and honesty are worried about their long-term survival, and this has only made investors more skittish. As they see stories like WeWork, Fast, and Bolt, investors are becoming less willing to "wait it out." Many are simply cutting their losses, admitting that their initial investment is gone, and refusing to put in another penny to the companies they've supported. They're worried. Everyone is worried.

In this climate, many founders are trying to pivot their companies to a more rational way of running, but it's not easy to pivot quickly. When I've spent time with founders who are trying to make that pivot, I've found that many of them have somewhere between four and six months of cash left in the bank. They have to make a change before the money runs out; but realistically, it's going to be incredibly difficult, especially when they are burning cash and not putting money back in the bank.

While four to six months might sound like a lot of time, it is in fact practically no time, and the sand seems to slip through the hourglass at an accelerated rate when the bank account is emptying. Often, the term sheets they are able to extract at this point are downrounds—and they almost always heavily dilute the founders, and even some of the original investors, to an egregious degree because it's clear that the founders have no choice but to accept terrible terms.

On the other hand, I know some founders who have raised very little or even no money—and their companies are not only growing quickly, but they're also actually quite profitable and fundamentally healthy compared to companies with much larger cash reserves. They are largely or entirely self-sustaining, so they don't continuously need to figure out how to get more cash in the bank. However, even these companies have to figure out how to manage their profitable businesses through these tough economic times.

So, both the self-sustaining companies *and* the companies who have been burning cash all along need to pivot their product or their messaging to survive times like the current economic climate. Many of them have gone through layoffs in an attempt to cut costs. I know of one company in my space that laid off people immediately after raising hundreds of millions of dollars. It seems unbelievable. How can a company raise $120 million and then immediately let sixty people go?

It is quite likely, as rumor has it, that the layoffs were actually a condition of the raise. The VCs, who are now starting to comport themselves in ways that look a lot more like private equity firms, looked at the company financials and said, "Yes, we will extend your runway and give you what you feel you need, but we expect you to behave yourselves more responsibly, stop burning through cash, and earn money in a more rational manner from now on."

All of these recent developments have made the go-to-market principles discussed in this book seem radically relevant, with true immediacy—but, of course, they were always relevant. The business world can always change without notice. We might see boom times in the coming months, or a turn to an even worse economic climate. You just never know.

One thing is certain. If we've learned anything from the cautionary tales that have come out of this entire period, it's that the companies who adhere to discipline around their bottom line and manage themselves in a more rational and scrappy way will enjoy higher valuations because they will be able to withstand sudden changes in the environment. The companies who comport themselves according to the principles shared in this book, even when they don't have to, are the ones who can thrive through all market conditions.

Introduction

The summer camp counselors handed each kid a single red paper-clip, loaded us all onto a bus, and drove us to an unsuspecting shopping mall in town. The game was called "Bigger and Better" (you may have heard of it as "the Paperclip Game"), and the rules were deceptively simple. We were supposed to find someone in the mall who would agree to trade our paperclip for a bigger and better item. Then, once we'd made a trade, we were supposed to take the new item and trade it with someone else for something even better.

We had one hour to continue making trades around the mall for progressively better items, and whoever came back with the biggest and most expensive item at the end of the hour was the winner. The one caveat was that we couldn't use any money. We had to start with just the paperclip and use only the items we traded for along the way. No bribes, no shortcuts, and no cheating.

They set us loose, and we fanned out across the mall. I made a beeline for the first friendly-looking woman I saw sitting on a bench near the mall fountain. After I explained the rules, she agreed to take my paperclip in exchange for a pencil from her purse. I thanked her before hastily running off to make another trade. The next few people I talked to brushed me off. However, I was determined. Eventually, a teenage girl in the food court agreed to take my pencil in exchange for a hair scrunchie.

As I raced around the mall making trades, I soon perceived a certain strategy to the game. If you want to win Bigger and Better, you can't take just any old trade that comes along. If you do, you might trade yourself into a dead end. For example, a single shoe might be worth more than a hair scrunchie, but nobody's going to want it—and it won't help you down the line. A kitten might be wonderful, but the number of people who would decide on the spot to adopt a pet is probably very limited. You have to keep building real, thoughtfully strategic value—not just to win, but simply to keep playing the game.

I refused many trades: chewed gum, a used sock, a ripped concert ticket for a performance that had already happened, and so on. Eventually, I traded the hair scrunchie for a candy bar. The candy bar led to a tiny stuffed animal from the mall arcade. The stuffed animal led to a baseball cap. By the end of the hour, I returned to the bus with a triumphant smile on my face, pushing a gently used child's pink BMX bicycle. Others came back with really impressive items, too: a small ladder, a pair of barbie dolls, and more. But I had won the game, and that experience has stuck with me all these years.

I had transformed a paperclip into a BMX bike in one hour without using any money or additional resources—not a bad hour's work for a twelve-year-old girl. Of course, I didn't go straight from the paperclip to the bike. It took a series of thoughtful steps as I increased the value of what I had, making it bigger and better one step at a time, with no money and at a very fast pace.

I learned that day that you can build value quickly through smart decisions and bold actions, even with the smallest of resources and no money. But how in the world does a childhood game like Bigger and Better apply to the business world?

In business, we usually assume there's a necessary tradeoff to small business growth: either your business can grow fast, or grow well, or it can grow on the cheap. They say you can have two out of three, but not all. The working theory is that if you want to grow quickly, you have to start with a massive amount of money and resources and top it off greatly along your journey. That often means giving up much more equity in your company to investors than you may feel comfortable doing.

It also means that, over time, you become increasingly indebted and/or diluted. At the extreme end of this spectrum, we witness companies like WeWork raising and then spending hundreds of millions of dollars to grow, only to achieve underwhelming results that hurt founders and investors unnecessarily. There's now a healthy backlash to this type of thinking.

As it turns out, it is simply not true that you must throw enormous amounts of money and resources at a growth plan in order to make it work. Just like that childhood game, you can grow a small business "from paperclip to bicycle" through a mindset of confidence and audacity—and, above all, some smart, strategic, and tactical actions. In the game, we only had an hour to grow the value of our paperclip. Similarly, in real life, paperclip-sized businesses don't usually have much time to grow if they want to survive. According to the Bureau of Labor Statistics, roughly 20 percent of all small businesses fail within the first year. Thirty percent of them fail by the end of the second year, and half fail by the end of year five. After a decade, the failure rate is a whopping 70 percent. And the ultimate failure rate is about 90 percent.[4]

That's right. Ninety percent of all small businesses eventually fail.

---

4   Georgia McIntyre, "What Percentage of Small Businesses Fail? (And Other Need-to-Know Stats)," *Fundera* (blog), last updated November 20, 20202, https://www.fundera.com/blog/what-percentage-of-small-businesses-fail.

Bear in mind, when we talk about small businesses, we're referring to companies with fewer than five hundred employees, so many businesses that don't think of themselves as small still fall into this category—and the bleak statistics still apply.

By the end of 2020, there were approximately 31.7 million small businesses in the country, making up 99.9 percent of all US businesses and over 47 percent of the working population.[5] It's fair to say that every single person in the country is involved either directly or indirectly with a small business, so this shocking failure rate touches everyone and has a dramatic impact on the nation's economy.

However, while statistics might be striking, they can't even begin to convey the real enormity of the problem in terms of lost livelihoods and wasted potential. On a personal level, it's excruciating to put so much of yourself into a business only to watch it wither and die despite your best efforts. These kinds of stories are happening every day across the country.

But they aren't the stories we like to tell in the business world, are they? No, we prefer to focus on the one-in-a-million success stories. We write books and articles about "how to become the next Google." The 31.7 million small businesses in this country don't need to know how to become the next Google—they need to know

---

5   https://cdn.advocacy.sba.gov/wp-content/uploads/2020/06/04144224/2020-Small-Business-Economic-Profile-US.pdf.

how to survive the early infancy stages of their company's existence so they can become thriving midsized companies.

Even those destined to become the Next Big Thing must first move through their infancy and survive into adulthood. Additionally, the backlash against outlandish investments like those made by SoftBank in WeWork and soberness about market fluctuations are driving all investors, including the venture capital world, toward an ever more grounded approach whereby the fundamentals of unit economics now matter more deeply than in the past.

Often, even when small companies do survive, the founders feel unnecessarily compelled to give away most of their ownership to investors—diluting not only themselves, but also any existing earlier investors in the process. That leaves founders with a difficult choice: Either 1) bootstrap (or raise money but very modestly) and die; or 2) raise lots of money, survive, but "die" as the effective owner of the company. It's kind of a depressing choice, isn't it?

It's like a game of golf where you are faced with an enormous sand trap on either side. On one side, there's a trap that leads to small business death. On the other side, there is the possibility of throwing lots of money at the project but ending up with very little equity in your company.

Is it possible to drive the golf ball down the very narrow path between them?

The answer is a resounding yes. Your small company can achieve dramatic growth in a very lean way without requiring you to give away more of the ownership of the business than absolutely necessary. How do I know this? Because I've seen it, I've helped to make it happen, and I've clarified the necessary steps for driving the golf ball between the sand traps.

A LEAN PATH TO SCALING QUICKLY

Imagine being more cash-stable, having much higher margins as a company, hanging on to more of your equity, and delivering more value to any investors you might have, all while building enterprise value. Imagine pouring more of your money into creating better products and services rather than dumping it all right back into paid marketing. After all, marketing costs are another sand trap for small businesses—a trap that they often don't know how to avoid.

There's a rule of thumb that says, "Never save money on marketing; save money elsewhere." This rule of thumb is false. It's possible to market phenomenally well without relying more than absolutely necessary on costly crutches. Paid marketing is effective and almost always necessary, but there's a minimum effective dose at any given time, and you can reduce that dose by thinking differently.

You don't have to spend so much on marketing that you have little left for improving your core deliverables. "But if we don't pay for more marketing," many think, "we won't get enough customers to survive. We have to put growth first."

What if it didn't have to be that way? What if you could spend less on marketing and more on creating better products? After all, marketing yourself is not your core deliverable. Shouldn't you focus your financial energy on what makes your company unique and compelling?

It's possible to do so, and to do it in a very lean way. The strategy depends on some mindset principles and a few key tactics, all of which are fully available to you even with very limited resources. In this book, I'm going to show you how.

First of all, the strategy maximizes non-transactional sales and marketing to build enterprise value using owned channels, which enables you to market even when you're cash-constrained, whether by choice or circumstance. That frees up more resources for developing products and improving your core deliverables. Since you're using owned channels, every penny you spend is "building your own house," not unlike paying a mortgage instead of paying rent. So when the going gets tough, you will still be able to market yourself.

This strategy also promotes radical generosity, giving lavishly to customers and other companies you partner with. Anyone can be radically generous, no matter how small the company or how few resources they possess, and there's almost always an immediate return. It turns out, when you give generously to others, they want to give back to you, and fast. It is counterintuitive, but it works.

I'll also show you how to position yourself as a thought leader at the center of your industry. Yes, even the smallest company in the world can become a central thought leader. It may seem a bit like Napoleon Bonaparte crowning himself emperor, but in reality, you do this by providing useful information that speaks to the particular needs of your customers, prospects, and "partners."

I know this strategy works because I've developed and used it myself. Over the course of my career, I've contributed to six exits of early-stage companies—most of which were minimally funded or entirely bootstrapped startups, and all in high-growth environments. In one recent instance, I helped lead a company where I implemented this very strategy, achieving virtually 10x growth in a three-and-a-half-year period, lifting annual recurring revenue (ARR) 1,500 percent, and growing earnings before interest, taxes, depreciation, and amortization (EBITDA) significantly with extremely limited resources and practically no outside funding—all of which led to a highly visible and spectacular exit when we were acquired by a competitor.

This exit would have been far less exciting had founders, investors, and employees become heavily diluted by raising more investment dollars than absolutely needed. It turns out, what matters most is leaping out of the perilous small-company pool where most companies end up perishing and into the bigger leagues—but in a way that preserves and grows value rather than burning cash.

So I'm not sharing tactics that are theoretical. I've seen how they can achieve outsized results in counterintuitive ways. This is a proven playbook, and if you're tasked with growth in a resource-constrained company, or if you just want to become more disciplined about your growth (i.e., growing fast without emptying your purse), then this book is for you. Since the strategy is counterintuitive, we'll start by addressing the mindset principles you need to embrace in order to make the most of it.

In the end, even with few resources and little to no outside funding, you should be able to punch above your weight class and achieve some massive victories and impressive growth at a breathtaking pace. I've seen it happen. I've helped make it happen, and now I want to do the same for you.

At the end of each chapter, I've included some key questions to help you take the various pieces of this growth strategy and customize them for your particular situation. The aggregate of your answers should, by the end of this book, provide you with an actionable plan for implementing this strategy in your own company.

PART ONE

Bigger & Better Mindset Principles

A Non-Transactional Approach

"I've learned that you shouldn't go through life with a
catcher's mitt on both hands; you need to be able to
throw something back... I've learned that people will
forget what you said, people will forget what you did,
but people will never forget how you made them feel."

—MAYA ANGELOU

I S IT REALLY POSSIBLE FOR A SMALL BUSINESS TO NOT only survive and thrive, but to actually grow and scale on a shoestring? The statistics are grim, and perhaps your own experiences as a small business leader have been discouraging. However,

I have personally witnessed and helped to refine a lean growth strategy that can help even the smallest resource-constrained company achieve remarkable growth, and it all begins by adopting a radically different mindset than most small business leaders currently possess.

Key to this new mindset is a non-transactional approach to the way you do business. What does a successful relationship with a customer look like from cradle to grave? In your typical transactional relationship, it starts with a lead, which results in a first conversation. Maybe the customer clicks on your Google ad. Whatever the case, that first conversation eventually leads to a first proposal and discussion about pricing, which hopefully results in a sale. The sale ideally leads to retention—a loyal customer who continues to buy from you—and that relationship continues until either they stop buying from you or you stop selling to them. We can represent the whole life cycle visually in Figure 1.

But what if there was a dramatically different approach, a non-transactional approach that changed everything, starting with the way they found you in the first place? What if, instead of finding you through a Google ad, they came to you through a different combination of factors, such as a warm referral related directly in some way to their needs, a warm partnership from within your industry, or a pre-existing awareness because you had somehow been providing value long before they ever became a customer?

Figure 1.

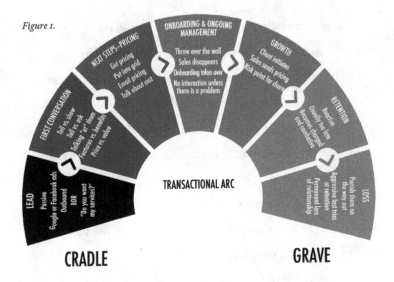

What if they were already prequalified and 60 percent of the way through your funnel because of thought leadership you'd provided them free of charge? Instead of through a Google ad *declaring* you a thought leader, what if a customer came to you already having predetermined that you're an authority through the generous value you'd already provided to them?

In a transactional approach, because there's very little pre-existing relationship with the customer, that first conversation is largely focused on qualifying the lead. Then, subsequent discussions focus on a salesperson persuading the customer into a sale. But what if you already had a relationship with a prospect, and that first conversation was more consultative than sales-oriented?

In a transactional approach, the next step is to create a proposal and offer your pricing; but what if, instead of offering pricing, you provided solutions—not just your own solutions, but potentially also solutions from other companies you'd created partnerships with? Let's suppose you're an e-commerce fulfillment company, and you realize that the customer needs an electronic data interchange (EDI) solution provider because they're going to start drop shipping for Macys.com. In a transactional approach, you might be forced to say, "Let us know once you've chosen and implemented an EDI provider, and we'll complete the deal."

In a non-transactional approach, you should already have warm partnerships with EDI providers, so you can say, "Hey, we understand you need an EDI solution provider. No matter what you choose to do regarding your choice of a fulfillment partner— whether you ultimately work with us or not— we can connect you with one."

Instead of simply trying to make a sale, you're acting almost like a consulting company trying to meet the customer's needs broadly. You have provided real value and guidance, establishing yourself as a true potential partner and a subject matter expert in your space. This will be impossible to ignore when the time comes for them to make their final decision on a provider, and because you are showing your value, you won't be in a price race to the bottom. At the same time, you're feeding your partners with leads which serve to deepen those relationships, all of which is going to pay you back down the road.

A FOCUS ON BUILDING RELATIONSHIPS

As company leaders, we all talk about how we want to give more, but with this approach, we don't have to wait until somebody has signed up as a customer to start giving to them generously. Instead, you're giving to them generously early and often—long before they speak to you directly. This is called *radical generosity*, and it's key to the growth strategy we're going to share in this book. (In fact, I devote an entire chapter to it.)

You're going to practice radical generosity not just with your prospects, but with all those around them, because you're making yourself part of their world. Long before you've given them a proposal, you're already becoming ultra-sticky by delivering value to them and to those around them.

And we're not talking about giving them a spreadsheet with your pricing on it. Instead, maybe you give them a gorgeous, beautifully designed solution book, like the kind you would get from a major consulting firm. Instead of meeting with them to conduct a pricing review, you're going to conduct a *solution* review, where you take the prospect through the entire solution, even including recommended third-party solutions from your network of partnerships.

With a non-transactional approach, you celebrate with your customer when they win. Sales doesn't just pass them to onboarding but remains in the picture, talking to them regularly, providing ongoing value, and learning about their next needs. You provide ongoing authority and thought leadership, giving them what they need from within your network.

In other words, you become the center of their world, because you're constantly in touch with them about what they need next. You're keeping your finger on the pulse and staying ahead of their needs by talking to them regularly. This is a crossover between sales, customer success, and account management that creates a continuum from onboarding to ongoing management to maturity to retention. It never stops. Indeed, that life cycle might look something like Figure 2.

Of course, you don't have forever, so even if you're really good at this, there's a finite lifetime value (LTV) to most customers. Someday, they will leave you, one way or another, so then the question becomes: how do you behave when a customer leaves? And what do you do *after* they leave? What you do as they leave and after they leave are just as important as what you do beforehand in a non-transactional approach. After all, many leads come through

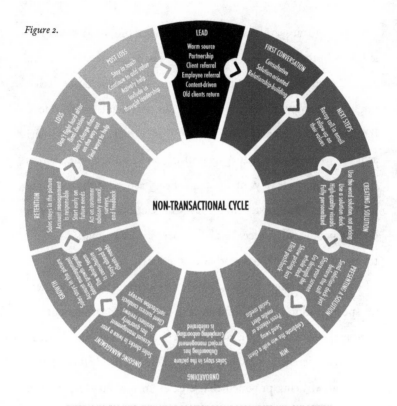

Figure 2.

THERE IS NO "GRAVE", EVEN YOUR LOSSES BECOME RESOURCES AND CAN RETURN.

referrals, and referrals don't have to stop just because a customer moves on. Moreover, sometimes customers do come back.

Imagine if you continued to treat a customer well on their way out and stayed in touch long after they were gone. There's no value in leaving their world, and if you continue to provide, they might come back. Even if they don't, they might speak well of you to others.

This non-transactional approach is focused on building relationships and providing value to prospects, customers, former customers, and even people who will never become customers. Some of that might seem counterintuitive, but it's a mindset that is going to feed into every other principle we discuss in this book. It's a differentiator for your business that costs nothing and can be applied across the entire life cycle of your company. Every aspect of the customer life cycle can be approached in a non-transactional way. When you do this, people will notice. You'll find people often remark, "You do things *very* differently from other companies."

Indeed, adopting a consultative relationship with customers, prospects, and former customers—providing value throughout the customer life cycle—often surprises people. Through social media, through conferences and white papers, there is a steady flow of valuable content being provided that creates an ongoing relationship with people long before they come to you, and long after they leave. And that non-transactional approach is merely the external face of the internal approach.

It doesn't matter what your industry has traditionally told you—you can choose to be non-transactional across every step of your interactions. At the core of this approach is a commitment to creating and maintaining a relationship by generously providing value to people no matter where they are in the customer life cycle. Done well, you can use this approach to position yourself at the very center of your industry.

"But we're a very small company," you might say. "Nobody is going to position us at the center of our industry. Nobody is going to view us as thought leaders."

It doesn't matter. You don't need anyone else's permission or approval. You can choose where your company sits within your industry through your own actions. You decide whether you're central to your industry or peripheral by the way you approach the customer life cycle and your industry as a whole. No one else decides. Whether you're sitting in the balcony and observing the action from a distance, or right down in the front row with the orchestra, is up to you.

How do you do this? Let's explore that question next.

Exercises to Build Your Playbook

———

- Is there some thought leadership you could provide to establish your authority and begin developing relationships with prospects long before they ever make contact with your company?

  _____

  _____

  _____

- How could you create a consultative relationship with customers, prospects, and former customers?

  _____

  _____

  _____

- Are there companies you could create warm partnerships with in order to send customers their way?

  _____

  _____

  _____

- How can you treat customers *after* they leave you in order to maintain the relationship and encourage referrals and recommendations?

_____

_____

_____

- Using the following template, create your own non-transactional cycle. How does each wedge translate to your specific business?

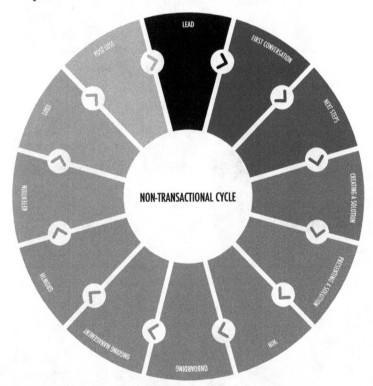

THERE IS NO "GRAVE", EVEN YOUR LOSSES BECOME RESOURCES AND CAN RETURN.

2

Be the Center of Your Industry

"Not all of us have power, but we all have influence. That is why we can each be leaders. The most important forms of leadership come not with position, title, or robes of office, not with prestige and power, but with the willingness to work with others to achieve what we cannot do alone....Always choose influence rather than power."

—RABBI LORD JONATHAN SAKS

BEFORE YOU CAN DECIDE WHAT INDUSTRY YOU'RE the center of, you have to decide what industry you're in. Pick something broad enough so that there's enough "meat on the bone" to take advantage of, and carefully consider the *total addressable market* (TAM). You want to pick an industry that's big enough that it matters whether or not you're the center of it. After all, being the center of the *universe* is more impressive than being the center of a very small closet.

It's a question of self-definition. What are you going to be the center of? This makes a huge difference. Perhaps the most famous example is found in the story of Smith Corona and IBM. Both were manufacturers of typewriters, but they positioned themselves in different industries. Smith Corona established itself as a manufacturer of typewriters, and consequently became obsolete along with that technology. By the 1990s, nobody cared if a company was the center of the typewriter industry.

But IBM positioned themselves as a tech solutions company, and they continued to play a dominant role in their industry. More than that, they continued to have relevance in the eyes of consumers long after Smith Corona was considered to be nothing more than a relic of a bygone era. The two companies were designing and manufacturing the same kind of products for years, but they positioned themselves in different industries, and it had a huge impact on their trajectories.

You have to decide what industry you're in before you can decide you're going to be the center of it. What is it that you do? Figure that out first. Then decide what industry you're going to be part of.

As we said, make sure you're at the center of something large enough that it matters.

For example, if you are with an e-commerce fulfillment company, you could place yourselves in the center of the e-commerce enablement world as a whole. Expand your scope to define yourselves as "e-commerce enablement" by showing how what you do—in this case, fulfillment—is at the center of e-commerce enablement.

The key to doing this is to continuously ask the question, "What does this mean to the customer?" When you do this, you look beyond what you do physically to what you mean to your customer: what are you actually allowing them to do?

By the way, it doesn't matter if your industry doesn't *currently* have any center, and it doesn't matter if you're *not* currently at the center. The point is to create a frame of reference for how you position yourself. Once you choose an industry, you also get to choose the criteria that will define your centricity. So, my company chose e-commerce enablement, an industry comprised of all of those companies that help other companies to sell and deliver their products online. Why? Because we realized that in many, if not most, ways we sat at the center, and that without us nothing could really happen.

It doesn't have to be one thing. It could be a number of things. For example, an e-commerce fulfillment business touches about 90 percent of the functionalities that are necessary in order to sell something online, so it was natural for my company to position itself in a way that showed how it was central to the entire e-commerce ecosystem.

"We make e-commerce possible!" Suddenly, we're at the center of e-commerce. We're not in fulfillment; we are in enablement! "We're an e-commerce enablement company, and we sit at the epicenter of the e-commerce ecosystem."

After all, nothing matters in e-commerce unless a product ends up on somebody's doorstep, and that alone made our company easy to position at the center. As I put it in a *Forbes* article on this subject, "No matter how you look at it, every aspect of e-commerce enablement is determined by the brand's fulfillment capabilities."[1]

In other words, you are, in a sense, creating a picture of yourself within your industry in which you are the hub and everything else connects to you like spokes on a wheel. Conduct the same thought experiment for your small business. What do you want to be at the center of, and how are you going to create a picture of your centrality to that industry?

Even if everything in your industry isn't plugged directly into what you do, there are countless ways to position yourself as the

---

1   Esther Kestenbaum Prozan, "Fulfillment Is at the Epicenter of E-Commerce Enablement," Forbes Business Council, *Forbes*, May 21, 2021, https://www.forbes.com/sites/forbesbusinesscouncil/2021/05/21/fulfillment-is-at-the-epicenter-of-e-commerce-enablement/?sh=6b5e7566113e.

hub. Maybe you're not the "be all and end all" deliverable of the industry, but you can place yourself somewhere on the critical path to industry success. Maybe without your product or service, everything else simply gets messed up. Maybe you deliver the end goal of your industry. There are a lot of ways to position yourself at the center of your industry, so think carefully.

Although complex in actuality, e-commerce fulfillment, practically speaking, is essentially little more than people putting products into packages and sending them on their way. It's a service that becomes so transparent that it could be dismissed fairly easily. But positioning yourself as the hub of your industry, and speaking of yourself that way both internally and externally, will enable you to dole out thought leadership wisdom that connects you to customers—as well as to a broad array of "partner" companies.

Identify a large, meaningful superset of entities in your industry and connect them to your company; this will drive your messaging across everything you do. You can do this even if you're a very small company. You might think, "What do I possibly have to give? My business is very small, and what we do feels tangential." That's just imposter syndrome rearing its ugly head. You're going to have to cast off these feelings of self-doubt and incompetence.

Clearly, you believe you have something to offer, or you wouldn't have started your business in the first place. Now, it's time to start sharing what you have to offer from a position of centrality—and you don't have to limit your target audience to other small companies. Dare to be "big-minded," even if you're very small.

Large is good, but narrowing down specificity can work in your favor, too. So, as you find a broad enough space, make sure that with your specific strengths within the larger industry, you choose an arena that you can own (if there is one). If you have some specific capability—say, you can work with products and deliverables that others cannot work with—you have the potential to fully or largely own a space.

Make sure to articulate that in your messaging, as well. In the fulfillment industry, there are huge players that can do things others cannot—some work with frozen and refrigerated goods, others with large and bulky items, and still others have the nuanced capabilities to handle complex apparel logistics. In each of these cases, small companies have leveraged these capabilities to make themselves indispensable to their more specific arenas and grown into entities that largely own their spaces.

REJECT IMPOSTER SYNDROME

It's natural for Jeff Bezos to talk big now, but it was a far bigger deal for him to talk big when he was selling books online and packaging them himself in his garage in 1994. That's the mindset you have to adopt. No matter how small your business is now, you have to see yourself and talk about yourself as if you're at the center of something very, very large. Let this attitude permeate everything you do. Build your products that way and share thought leadership that way. Do everything with that idea in mind.

Do you suppose Jeff Bezos ever felt imposter syndrome when he was just selling books out of his garage? Almost certainly. It's a part of human nature that most of us struggle with at some point. But he didn't speak about Amazon in small-minded terms. In fact, he had much bigger dreams and saw his company as the center of something truly visionary.

As he said in an interview in 1997, "I picked books as the first best product to sell online, making a list of—like—twenty different products that you might be able to sell. Books were great as the first best, because books are incredibly unusual in one respect: that is that there are more items in the book category than there are items in any other category by far... So, when you have that many items, you can literally build a store online that couldn't exist any other way."

He then added, "What's really incredible about this is that this is day one—this is the very beginning." And he concluded by saying, "I think, millennia from now, people will look back and say,

'Wow, the late twentieth century was really a great time to be alive on this planet.'"[2]

Do you see how he is positioning his little book-selling website as central to something huge and historic? This is the kind of mindset we're talking about. Even a small company can position itself as central, even *necessary*, to a very crowded space. Maybe you haven't invented something new. Maybe your product is something everyone has seen before. Again, using one of my favorite examples, everyone had seen e-commerce fulfillment before. It's a crowded space. Even so, it is possible to redefine the way people look at you by speaking differently, acting differently, and doing things none of your competitors do. The company's leadership needs to think, "Even if we never become a $10 billion company, that doesn't make us any less central to our industry."

For that reason, because of that attitude, you wind up aiming higher and reaching farther. In my experience, your amazing growth as a small business all starts with your self-image. Do you think you matter? Do you think you're worthy and able to be a lynchpin in an industry? Your self-image is going to play a central role in the

---

2   Isobel Asher Hamilton, "Jeff Bezos Is Stepping Down as Amazon's CEO. A Video of a Young Bezos from 1997 Shows Why He Decided to Build His Empire on Books." Insider, last updated February 3, 2021, https://www.businessinsider.com/1997-jeff-bezos-amazon-empire-viral-video-books-2019-11.

actions you take, the value you provide, the goals you set, and the thought leadership you share.

What you become will be largely shaped by what you think of yourself. Amazon didn't fumble its way to huge growth. It began with the audacious image Jeff Bezos had of his company even in the very early days. He positioned his tiny book-selling e-commerce business at the center of an industry that was poised to change the world, and that self-image drove the actions his company took in the decades to come. It drove the way he talked about Amazon and emboldened him to make audacious requests and take big steps forward.

It all starts when you figure out how to answer the following question: what do you want to be at the center of, and how are you going to create a picture of your centrality to that industry?

Exercises to Build Your Playbook

- What industry do you want to be at the center of, and how can you create a picture of your centrality to that industry?

  _____

  _____

  _____

- Can you position your small business in a way that touches most of your industry (like the hub in a wheel)? Draw that hub and the spokes. What factors put you at the center? Who radiates out to form the ecosystem of which you are central—which sub-industries and companies?

  _____

  _____

  _____

- How could you be "big-minded" in the way you talk about your company and what you have to offer?

  _____

  _____

  _____

- Within the broader industry, is there a specialty you have, and can you imagine largely owning that space? If so, what is that space, and why would you be the one to own it?

_____

_____

_____

- What do you provide that the market is otherwise lacking without you?

_____

_____

_____

3

Radical Generosity

"Juggling is about throwing, not catching. That's why it's so difficult to learn how to juggle....Paradoxically, if you get better at throwing, the catches take care of themselves."

—SETH GODIN

EVEN AS A SMALL, RESOURCE-CONSTRAINED COMpany, you have a lot more to give than you realize. Imagine if your company was an open-source platform for good things, giving constantly in surprisingly generous ways to prospects, customers, former customers, and even other companies. Think about how that would shape the image people have of you.

I grew up in a warm Hasidic community in Brooklyn, where I was raised in the Orthodox Jewish faith. Though I am no longer

Orthodox, the beautiful communal experience left me with some enormous life lessons about the bi-directional benefits of practicing radical generosity. People in my community were always willing to help one another, to meet needs, and to share what they had.

People practiced generosity for its own sake, not insisting upon a reward, because it tied into their values of community responsibility, being part of something larger than themselves, and the belief that all individuals in the community were interdependent. If you view your industry as a community, you can see this same sense of interdependence. There's a term used primarily in the tech world, called "interoperability," that refers to the ability of computer systems or software to exchange information.

Interoperability is a desirable quality for any software product, and it's why open application programming interfaces (APIs) and software development toolkits (SDKs) exist. Platforms and developer tools that enable applications to communicate and interact with each other make it far easier for businesses to bring together and integrate multiple tools for common purpose. Indeed, beyond software and apps, interdependence has become a core reality of the business world. Think, for example, of all the different apps, tech tools, and services you use in an ordinary work week just to do business. You need them to all play nicely together, at the very least, but ideally you want them all to integrate seamlessly and even contribute to one another.

That kind of interdependence was an essential reality of the Hasidic community of my childhood, where we believed that everything we possessed, both tangible and intangible, existed for the service of others in practical ways. Radical generosity was simply a way of life, and it worked from the inside out. First, and most importantly, you were radically generous with your family and closest friends. Then you were radically generous with your neighbors. Finally, you were radically generous with the community as a whole.

Like a series of concentric circles, you started with the people closest to you in life, and then gradually extended that generosity outward to ever broader circles. It was the reverse of those people who are really nice to strangers and people in need who they don't know, but dismissive and rude to their own loved ones.

The inside-out approach to radical generosity in the Hasidic community was never a "pie in the sky" practice. It was a very practical approach and lifestyle. If you had a car, or a wedding gown, or power tools that someone needed to borrow, you lent them without question. That's just how it was. Everything you had was available to be borrowed by family, friends, and neighbors; and everything they had was available to you.

It went beyond personal possessions. If you possessed a skill, like medical knowledge or the ability to change a tire, you offered it to the community on a voluntary basis. If you knew someone who wanted to get married, you set them up with somebody nice. If you knew of a job opening, you made a professional connection for someone who would be a good fit.

One of the most impressive aspects of this radical generosity among the community of my childhood had to do with sharing knowledge. As soon as you learned something, you immediately began teaching it to others. You didn't have to wait until you got your PhD or a formal position in a company. This intellectual generosity started early, so if you were five years old and you'd just learned the first letters of the Hebrew alphabet, you could and would turn right around and teach them to someone else.

This radical generosity appeared in so many ways. When someone died, the grieving family received free meals from friends and neighbors. Bear in mind, generosity had nothing to do with how wealthy you were. The way they looked at it, everyone had something to give, and you could always find ways to be generous by meeting needs, teaching, and sharing what you had.

I believe there's an incredible business lesson in this, and it comes down to your self-image. When you view yourself as small and insignificant, then you feel like you have very little to offer; as a result, you offer very little. But when you start thinking of yourself as bigger, you *become* bigger. You give more, share more, and create more value.

The amazing thing is—and I've seen this time and time again—when you give generously, you get back tenfold sooner or later (usually sooner, and often with blinding speed). In a sense, giving is its own reward, because it feels great to help others, but there's this amazing thing that happens when you become generous: people start giving you stuff in return almost immediately. People like to repay and reward those who have given to them, and in my experience, what they pay back is almost always bigger than what was given in the first place.

This is exactly what I experienced in companies where leadership modeled this kind of generosity. First, we began providing free consultations with customers about aspects of their businesses that had nothing to do with our core service. Then, we began pointing people in the directions of companies we'd partnered with. We could have said, "Let other companies find their own customers," but we didn't. We sent people their way, and we did it more and more. The response was incredible.

I've seen that it's possible to conduct events where half a dozen competing companies happily participate. People wonder, "How in the world can you get your competitors to attend the same event?" In great part, the answer is that they want to somehow repay you and stand with you because of your historic generosity with each of them.

When you create partnerships with other companies, always try to give 100 percent more than you take from them. The key is to not wait. Don't just sit around and wait for opportunities. And don't keep score focused on what "they" gave you. "We've given this much. How much have they given us?" Rather, practice the reverse: keep score focused on what *you* have given *them*.

I was once in a group facilitation where four hundred people simultaneously learned how to juggle. We were all given a few pins and asked to give it a try. As we began our attempts, pins flew everywhere, rolling under chairs and down corridors. People were chasing them down and trying over and over again in frustration.

After five to ten minutes, the facilitator addressed the crowd and gave us one insight that transformed everything. "Stop worrying about catching the pins," she said. "Catching is automatic. When someone throws a ball in your general direction, your arm automatically reaches out and catches it. It requires no thought. Focus on the throw, and the catch will take care of itself. Throw over and over again; get the throwing right. If you do that, the catches will naturally happen."

We did this—and it worked. Within ten minutes, the entire room, all four hundred of us, were successfully juggling. "Focus on the throw, and the catch will take care of itself" comes from a famous quote by Seth Godin. Here is the quote in full:

Juggling is about throwing, not catching.

That's why it's so difficult to learn how to juggle. We're conditioned to make the catch, to hurdle whatever is in our way to save the day, to—no matter what—not drop the ball.

If you spend your time and energy and focus on catching, it's inevitable that your throws will suffer. You'll get plenty of positive feedback for the catches you make, but you'll always be behind, because the throws you manage to make will be ever less useful.

Paradoxically, if you get better at throwing, the catches take care of themselves.

The only way to get better at throwing, though, is to throw. Throw poorly, throw again. Throw well, throw again. Get good at throwing first.[3]

Often, it is used to explain the value of doing the work without thinking about the outcome. The outcome is...well...an outcome(!) if you do the work. But I believe it is also about putting things out there in the world generously without worrying heavily about what the outcome will be—without worrying about what you will get back in return. Taking is automatic. When someone gives us something, we accept it with no problem, so focusing on

---

3   Seth Godin, *Poke the Box: When Was the Last Time You Did Something for the First Time?* (The Domino Project, 2011): 53.

the taking is futile. Focus on the throw, the giving, and the taking will take care of itself.

Just let it all pour out. Give without thinking about receiving. Give everything you have to give, trusting that it will all come back tenfold in one way or another—because it almost certainly will. It's going to come back to you faster than you expect. Indeed, people will fall all over themselves trying to give back to you because of the things you've done for them and the value they have derived.

Much of the time, what you give them costs *you* nothing but provides *them* everything. After all, what does it cost to send a customer referral to another company if they have a solution to meet a need that you simply can't meet? Bear in mind, you're not giving them money. You're not becoming some strange no-return investment firm. In fact, most of the time, what people really need is something other than money. They need advice to overcome a challenge, or they need some expertise that they lack, or they need to make a connection with a customer who is a good fit, or they need to hire.

Maybe it's an individual who needs a job, and you know of a perfect opening at another company. Indeed, that creates a feeling of indebtedness on both sides, because the individual will be grateful for the job, and the company will be grateful that you made a connection with a good hire.

The gratitude that the person feels will linger long after the job starts. Even as their career evolves, as they go from role to role, or company to company, over the coming decades, you will always have a halo and angel wings in their eyes. They'll never forget the generous thing you did for them once upon a time. You can't put a dollar value on something like that, because the opportunities for reciprocity go on and on.

The fact that most forms of radical generosity cost you nothing means that you can practice it no matter how small you are. You can move mountains for people in ways that are priceless, and it won't take anything away from you. It might cost a little bit of time and focus, and that can indirectly translate into money, but the results are incredible and well worth it.

When you do something nice for someone outside of the public arena, suddenly they are singing your praises everywhere they go, both privately and publicly. There is no form of targeted marketing that could ever achieve this—not as quickly, consistently, credibly, or immediately.

One reason why relationships sometimes break down is because everyone is waiting for what they're going to get back rather than just giving as much as they can. This is certainly true of business relationships. What I'm advocating is a form of generosity that gives and gives without waiting for repayment.

I was once challenged on this point by the CRO of another company who said, "Esther, that's all good and well, but you can't throttle that. I can throttle paid search—if I need leads, I put in money and leads result." Not true. When you create these kinds of generous "partnerships" with other organizations and the people within them, you can throttle them as needed in a way you never can with anything else in business. When you've been radically generous and you have a need, you can make those calls, and people will literally fight over who gets to help you. We'll dive deeper on this in our chapter on partnerships.

CREATE AN OPEN PLATFORM

We'll talk more about how you tactically practice radical generosity in upcoming chapters, but for now, I want you to begin wrapping your mind around the attitude this requires of you. Imagine putting out everything you have as an open platform. For example, I have seen companies launch collaborative industry organizations that operate much like trade associations, but with no monetization whatsoever.

I have seen hundreds of member companies sign on, with some of the biggest companies in the world signing on not just as members but to serve on various boards and councils. To make this work as a form of radical generosity, salespeople should never be involved, and the stated purpose should be to provide a platform for your industry where companies can work on things that matter to them. The organization or consortium should be an open-source think tank.

You can see how this not only promotes radical generosity, but also places your company at the center of the industry, as we discussed in Chapter One. What did you get out of it? Well, to be clinical, it extends your funnel on the front end. One of the challenges of outbound marketing is timing. You might have a giant list of prospects, and you can start at the top of that list calling them one at a time. However, you have no idea when each of the people on that list will have a need.

Another way to do this is to provide a tool that helps prospective companies in a way that then creates an ongoing dialogue between you and them. Perhaps it's a benchmarking or optimization tool that allows them to gauge how they are currently doing from a perspective meaningful to your space—and reveals how much better they could be doing, along with where the opportunities for optimization and improvement exist.

There will be some moment in time when a prospect needs what you're selling, and they're ready to buy from you, but getting the timing just right is incredibly difficult. You can't just call a prospect every single day and say, "Are you ready now?" However, what if you became a constant presence in their lives by continually delivering value to them? That way, the moment they have a need and are ready for a solution, you're already there. You've been there all along.

"Hey, that business has been giving me this great stuff for the past five months. I think they can meet our need right now."

It's like a benevolent and generous Trojan horse. Additionally, through generous partnerships with other companies, like an industry organization, partners are directing people to you who have a need that you can solve when they're ready for a solution.

Consider the following potential storyline, which I have seen happen: You begin creating thought leadership conferences and invite the chief commercial officer of one of your largest customers to be on a panel at one of your events, even though they were in no way related to decision-making regarding your products or services. After the event, you stay in touch with them and talk periodically about business and the industry. They move companies and become part of the C-suite for a huge conglomerate that is taking over 40 percent of the market share in a major category. You continue to talk once a month about your families, industries, all sorts of things. And then, one day, their company has a need, and because of your existing relationship with them, they recommend your company as their solution.

"I know these guys from past experience," they say. "You *have* to work with them."

We went through a request for proposal (RFP) process with the company and faced the thousand-pound gorilla in our space, and we beat them to the finals. It was a true David and Goliath story, and it wouldn't have been possible if we hadn't continued to talk to and listen to a former customer. It was radical generosity—and positioning ourselves at the center of our industry, as well—and it's a perfect example of why my small company experienced 10x growth.

There is nothing cynical about this—it is relationship-building of the highest order. You provide value for years while expecting nothing specific in return, and when the moment of need comes, you will be the one who has always been there.

In the coming chapters, we'll look at some ways to practice radical generosity, but I've seen firsthand the profound role this one mindset has on the growth of a small business with limited resources—more, perhaps, than anything else.

Ultimately, at the very least, it keeps you close to customers and prospects; and that, in turn, helps you stay ahead of their needs, which we will discuss next.

Exercises to Build Your Playbook

- How could you create an open platform for collaborating with other organizations in sharing thought leadership?

  _____

  _____

  _____

- What do you have that you can give on an ongoing basis?

  _____

  _____

  _____

- How can you become a constant presence in the lives of prospects by continually delivering value to them?
  - Tools?

    _____

    _____

    _____

- Content and thought leadership?

_____

_____

_____

- Events?

_____

_____

_____

4

Future-Proofing Your Customers' Needs

"You cannot escape the responsibility of
tomorrow by evading it today."
—ABRAHAM LINCOLN

YOU'VE PROBABLY HEARD THE FAMOUS QUOTE from Wayne Gretzky, but I hope you will bear with me as I mention it again here. As the legendary hockey player put it, "A *good* hockey player plays where the puck is. A *great* hockey player plays where the puck is going to be."

We live in a world where everyone is moving fast, so you have to intentionally stay ahead of where they're going to be or they'll leave you behind—whether that is related to lead sources, product capabilities, technology, locations, or something else. For example, if you have a robust lead source from your partnerships, a large percentage of your pipeline will come from referrals from those business partnerships.

In my career, I have seen situations where leads from significant partners have begun to falter. Your company needs to be alert and take steps to future-proof yourselves and your pipeline. If the nature of a partnership involves paying each other royalties for customer referrals, but the partner's payments begin showing up late, you would be right to worry that it could be a sign of trouble. They could be in trouble as a company, and then what happens to your lead source?

If you see the symptoms and act quickly on your observations, you can avoid disruptions to your pipeline. You can immediately start proactively diversifying your partnership base to fill the potential future gap in your pipeline and lessen the positive income of this faltering partner in your projections. Moreover, you must take their decline as a lead source into account as you do your financial modeling. But you must act early, because it takes time to rebuild such a source.

Perhaps you have noticed a trend where your biggest customers are really growing fast. That is a sign that they may need you to be able to work with more sophisticated software systems. It could be a big potential problem—and you need to move quickly, since it takes time to upgrade your systems or integration capabilities.

When a scaling company outgrows their current systems, they often need to be integrated into a full-scale ERP system (e.g., SAP or NetSuite) rather than stitching together numerous types of software for various functions. Make sure to stay ahead of their needs. Rather than waiting for your big customers to jump ship, upgrade what is needed. This will preemptively fill a potentially huge hole in your revenue stemming churn. Not only can you avoid losing your biggest customers, but you can also ensure that you will continue to meet their needs during future growth.

You can future-proof your business if you listen for the soft early signals and act on them with urgency.

LISTENING CLOSELY

Ultimately, staying ahead of your customers' future needs is about listening closely to what they're saying, paying attention to problems so you can take action. Customers may not tell you directly, "You guys don't have the type of integration we need, so we're thinking about leaving." However, if you stay in close touch with them and listen all along, you can perceive the problem as it arises, which enables you to take preemptive action to stay ahead of it.

Some of the actions you take to meet future customer needs will be quick, while others may take a very long time, so the relationship needs to be there constantly. For example, SAP integration can take anywhere from six to twelve months to create, and then it has to be certified, validated, and tested. Therefore, it is important for you to pick up on the earliest demand signals from your customers and begin implementing the solution as soon as possible.

Listen and look for those soft early demand signals and act on them long before they become an imminent problem. To do that, sometimes you have to take risks, because solutions can consume time and resources. Creating a way to integrate SAP or NetSuite was expensive for us and required a whole lot of decisions and resources. How tragic would it be if you waited too long, not giving yourselves enough lead time, and found yourselves just in the middle of figuring things out when your valued customers decided to bail for lack of ERP support?

Sometimes, you just have to take an educated guess and move fast on a solution when you perceive a future customer need. Dragging your feet to avoid risk can cost you customers, or even cause you to miss out on the evolution of your entire industry. Evolving customer needs are sometimes indications of industry-wide trends, after all.

According to a study by Bain & Company, increasing your customer retention rate by 5 percent will increase your profits by 25 to 95 percent.[4] Additionally, it's five to twenty-five times more expensive to acquire a new customer than to retain an existing one. And retention is about a lot more than just your actual deliverables. Indeed, churn is often the result of customers outgrowing a product or service provider, which cuts into your stackable revenue and customer LTV. For that reason, it's important to be forward-looking, not just focused entirely on meeting present needs, but also trying to peer into the future.

ADVISORY COUNCILS

One way to stay ahead of future needs is to create customer and partner advisory councils, which give you real input into what your industry is going to want next. An advisory council is a group of people from companies or organizations who are meaningful stakeholders in your company's success. They are gathered together for a voluntary term of service at the invitation of the company to provide advice and feedback that will help the company improve.

The idea is to ask these people, "What would you like us to be doing?" The participants have no active decision-making power in your company. They're just there to help you become a better

---

4   Amy Gallo, "The Value of Keeping the Right Customers," *Harvard Business Review*, October 29, 2014, https://hbr.org/2014/10/the-value-of-keeping-the-right-customers.

company so you can future-proof yourself. This is just one example of how you can be constantly finding ways to listen and learn from customers, prospects, partners, and others in order to get a sense of future needs, so you can "play where the puck is *going* to be."

Through advisory councils, not only do you get incredible feedback to help you perceive future needs for your industry and customers, but you also get an incredible marketing tool through implied testimonials and good will. Plus, it should cost you almost nothing to bring people together and listen to them.

Here are some ways to ensure success:

Don't Make It a Vanity Project

It's easy to pull together a panel of people who make you look good, but it's a meaningless project if all you get is praise. Be genuine about wanting to get real advice and feedback. This isn't as easy as it sounds. You have to be prepared to hear both praise and tough feedback. That means including people you know are likely to be candid, actively encouraging radical feedback, and sharing both wins and challenges with your advisory council members. This can make you feel vulnerable, but taking the leap of faith will help you reap the dual rewards: you'll get valuable input that will make your company better, and you'll develop a closer and more authentic relationship with a group of your key stakeholders.

Define the Constituent Groups and Consider Having More than One Council

Think about your company and then group the stakeholders into constituencies. These can be very direct relationships, like customers or partners, or more indirect and generalized, like people from organizations more broadly related to your industry. Also, think about whether you'd like them all in one council or whether it makes more sense to have, for example, a customer advisory council and a separate partner advisory council if their values and priorities are somewhat different.

Ensure a Varied and Representative Mix of Companies and People

Choose companies that range in size, vertical, geography, and more. Your council should be representative of the constituency as a whole. The same holds true for the specific people involved. Include people of differing roles, executive levels, and personalities. The more varied the voices are, the more valuable the collective input will be.

Assign Internal Ownership for the Council Initiative

Don't let this become an "orphan" project. Assign strong leadership to own the council initiative and the relationship, process, planning, and events. Choose natural leaders who are closest to the subject matter. For a customer advisory council, choose the person in your company who is the voice of the customer, like your VP of customer success. For your partner advisory council, choose your VP of partnerships.

Make Meetings Count

Prepare for your meetings and share an agenda in advance. Include guest speakers who can update people on what is new since the last meeting. Do demos of new technology, show videos of new locations or functions, and ask for real input.

Staying ahead of future needs means more than just thinking about the next quarter. You need to be looking well beyond, and not just for your biggest customers. Try to listen carefully to your mid- and small-sized customer companies, as well. Otherwise, you might not hear about some of the major changes that you need to prepare for.

Preparing for future needs is certainly a mindset, but it's also a discipline that must be ingrained in every part of your company.

Exercises to Build Your Playbook

- What are some ways that you can make sure you're listening to soft early demand signals from your customer so you can identify imminent problems?

  _____

  _____

  _____

- Consider creating an advisory council composed of companies or organizations who are meaningful stakeholders in your company's success and who can provide advice and feedback. What are these stakeholder groups?

  _____

  _____

  _____

- Create a list of five to seven organizations you would like to include in a customer advisory council. Do the same for a partner advisory council. Now, insert the names of the people from each organization you would like to include.

  _____

  _____

_____

_____

- For each council, draft an agenda for the first quarterly meeting you would like to hold.

_____

_____

_____

5

Discipline

"Self-respect is the fruit of discipline; the sense of
dignity grows with the ability to say no to oneself."
—ABRAHAM JOSHUA HESCHEL

FAST GROWTH AND DISCIPLINE AREN'T NATURAL
partners. When you're a small company, you need to grow
fast in order to survive, so you generally want to say yes to
everything—but that's not the way to achieve growth. Therefore,
you're going to have to instill some discipline in everything you do.
Things can change quickly for a small business, and sometimes you
have to make adjustments to the way you do business. Even then,
you still need to have some disciplined policies and procedures in
place to ensure you're moving in the right direction.

Creating policies and procedures is rarely the problem. It's having some degree of fidelity to them that becomes a challenge. What often happens is that policies get put in place, and then everything becomes an exception to the rule. You set guidelines, and then you betray them both internally and externally.

The main problem with betraying your own policies and procedures is that you lose moral authority. For example, let's suppose you set an internal policy for the target customers you're going to go after. This is entirely your decision. You get to choose who you're going after, so you set your target audience and train your marketing and sales teams.

Then you get out there in the marketplace, and your small company desperately needs money. You're young, poor, and struggling, and it becomes very easy to betray that policy and just start trying to reach anybody you can.

"We just need to make some sales, no matter who they come from."

Of course, you can change a policy when you need to, though what tends to happen is that the policy remains, but the external behavior goes against it. Suddenly, you are saying internally that you're going to focus on a specific target audience, but externally, you just try to reach anyone you can.

Why does this matter? Because phenomenal growth is almost always a product of a clear direction, and moving in a clear direction *requires* discipline.

THE DOWNSTREAM IMPACT
OF CONFLICT AVOIDANCE

In the e-commerce fulfillment industry, for example, most providers have guidelines about the inventory they receive from customers. They have to meet certain standards in order for them to be received and prepared for shipping, and that means they have to be packed in a certain way and barcoded. They are not supposed to be sent haphazardly by customers to the fulfillment center. In fact, most fulfillment companies have an entire document to make these guidelines very clear and accessible.

When a customer signs the master services agreement, they agree to follow those guidelines; but all too often, when they send their very first shipment, it's a big mess. They've agreed to the guidelines, then immediately behaved as if the guidelines didn't exist. This isn't due to ignorance. Usually, salespeople or onboarding staff have explained the requirements, and customers have gone through an onboarding process. Still, that first shipment will arrive upside down, jammed together, with no regard to any semblance of order, much less the guidelines.

On the other hand, we know that companies betray their very own guidelines all too often. Instead of kicking the shipment back to the customer, the people on the ground may roll their eyes and say, "Okay, fine, let's try to do this anyway." However, it ends up taking ten times as long to get all of the products packed properly and shipped. Worse than that, by not sending the package back, companies are teaching their customers that the guidelines were mere suggestions rather than actual requirements all along.

In such cases, even if they'd decided to go ahead and ship the first package, they should have called the customer and said, "You sent this to us incorrectly. We'll go ahead and ship it this one time, but we really need you to follow the guidelines in the future." Instead, often companies will go ahead and pack it, do it poorly, and never even tell the customer about it. So, in the end, they don't even get the emotional credit for going out of their way to serve the customer. On the contrary, because it takes longer, customers end up liking them less. No good deed goes unpunished.

Thus, tolerating the subversion of standards has no upside. Nothing positive comes from it. What starts as a simple lack of discipline—"Oh, I'm just going to work with this anyway, even though it breaks our own policies"—has enormous downstream effects. When you're spending far more time on a task than you should, you're not working on the next task, so you're affecting other customers. It's a domino effect that can slow down your growth for a long time to come.

If you calculated what this lack of discipline is costing you, the result would be astronomical. Conflict avoidance makes a deep impact on your revenue—and not in a good way. No one wants to be the tough person who insists on the policies, but if you do, you'll reap rewards quickly. A lack of discipline, no matter what form it takes, costs you hard dollars and robs you of some opportunities that you might otherwise have. You inevitably waste time making up for your lack of discipline, which robs you of productive time you could be spending on doing more for your business. This is a much bigger problem when you're operating with severely limited resources.

A small business only has so much in terms of dollars, human resources, and bandwidth, so when you're not disciplined in one area, it tends to impact everything else. Most of what we talk about in the next part of this book requires discipline in order to really make it work. I want to be clear: the growth that my company achieved was the result of a certain mindset, some smart strategies, and a *whole lot of discipline*. Once you set the right direction, you have to stick with it until further notice.

As a small business, it can be very tempting to cut corners, let people get away with things, and betray your own policies and procedures. You want to avoid conflict with customers. You want to say *yes* to everything. But the downstream effect of these decisions can kill your potential.

FINDING THE RIGHT FITS

One of the most difficult areas to create and maintain discipline in is customer alignment. It's really easy to decide in the boardroom who your ideal avatar is, but sticking with it when you're "in the field" is stressful and hard. When you really need money, it's tempting to just try to reach out to anyone who will take your hand, but creating customer alignment is one of the most important tactics for achieving growth in a resource-constrained organization.

The same goes for the people you hire. The mindset principles that drive your company are going to have a bigger impact on what you do than anything else will, and they should be at the heart of how you hire people. Indeed, one of the best decisions I've made was to start hiring people *for their mindset* more than anything else.

In another company I worked for, we hired an individual who, on the surface, seemed like a perfect fit. He had exactly the right trade knowledge, knew all the jargon, and required very little training. Bringing him on board felt like a "plug and play" situation, so hiring him was a no-brainer.

The perfect fit did not last long before problems became obvious. While he had the right knowledge and experience, his mindset was so wrong for our company that it was like he came from a completely different world. There was nothing wrong with him personally. He was a good, hard worker, and a decent person. He also had a good track record at selling in his previous company, but the way he thought about things was just very different from the mindset we'd adopted and cultivated. Within about ten days, he struggled to get along with coworkers, and nobody liked him.

Ultimately, he just didn't fit well with the mindset of the company, and it hindered him from really being successful there. It also contributed negatively to our overall growth and direction.

If the mindset is wrong, even the most qualified candidate is going to struggle at your company. This individual brought his own Rolodex, but he struggled with the idea of punching above our weight class, and he wasn't comfortable being held to very high standards with very low resources. This kind of thinking was completely foreign to him, and in fact, he felt insulted by it.

"How dare you not provide me with the resources I need?" he asked. "You're setting me up to produce less than everybody else! In my old company, I had plenty of money for delivering sales lists."

Ultimately, you need to find stakeholders who not only understand your company's mindset, but also enjoy it. It feels gamified to them, so they get up every morning and revel in it. This needs to be central to the conversation during their interview. People need to know exactly the mindset they'll be asked to embrace, so they have every opportunity to get up and leave before they enter into a company culture that they cannot wrap their minds around.

To avoid making the same hiring mistake, we had to begin clarifying to all interviewees that our marketing budget was purposefully very controlled, our expectations very high, and our approach very non-transactional. We also began asking situational questions, because sometimes a person will say they understand your mindset even though, in practical terms, they don't know how to embrace it.

For example, we began asking questions like, "You're going to have a much smaller budget here, so how will you achieve the same or greater results? If we gave you half the budget you had at your previous company, how would you feel about it? Would you feel resentful, or would you see it as a fun challenge?" And so on.

Really get to the heart of a candidate's mindset principles and see how comfortable they appear to be with your own mindset. In this instance, it sometimes served us better to work with people from scrappy companies, even if they had less experience or required a bit more training; but counterintuitively, we also found people from large corporations with truly entrepreneurial mindsets.

Beyond hiring the right stakeholders with the right mindset, you need to continue cultivating those mindset principles throughout your organization and reinforcing them every day. Drive this as a leader for your entire company, creating constant awareness of them through your words and actions. If you bring someone on board who really "gets" your mindset and feels genuinely excited about it, then they will truly be a "plug and play" stakeholder who will thrive from day one and can be cultivated to evangelize the mindset to others, as well.

The mindset principles we've talked about in part of a non-transactional approach—being the center of your industry, radical generosity, and staying ahead of future needs—underpin all the tactics that we'll talk about in Part Two. It's incredibly important that you find people who can embrace the principles, and also that you cultivate those principles in your existing people. Indeed, I would even dare to say that hiring for the right mindset is better than hiring for the right experience or skills.

By now, you should have an idea of the right mindset that you need, so we're ready to dive into some tactics that transform those principles into concrete action.

Exercises to Build Your Playbook

———

- Do you have disciplined policies and procedures in place throughout your organization to ensure you're moving in the right direction? What are three areas where you could use more discipline, policies, and procedures?

  _____

  _____

  _____

- Are there ways you are betraying your own guidelines under the guise of customer convenience or for other reasons? List the ways you see yourself doing this. How can you stop doing this?

  _____

  _____

  _____

- What interview questions can you put into your hiring process to ensure you hire stakeholders with the right mindset principles? List two or three situational questions you can ask in your next interview.

  _____

  _____

_____

_____

- What are some ways that you can continue cultivating mindset
  principles throughout your own organization and reinforce
  them every day?

_____

_____

_____

PART TWO

Bigger & Better Tactics

6

Creating Customer
Alignment

*"Consistent alignment of capabilities and internal
processes with the customer value proposition
is the core of any strategy execution."*
—ROBERT S. KAPLAN

WHEN IT COMES TO DRIVING THE 10X GROWTH of your small company, there is one very important tactical decision that is key: who is the right customer? For some business-to-business (B2B) customers, it is important to go after ever-larger customers. As it turns out, bigger customers are more likely to survive to maturity so that they churn less. That means you get to enjoy the full blossoming of your existing customer relationships, including stackable revenue that produces a dramatic growth curve.

Even if you are Software-as-a-Service (SaaS) and don't have a subscription-based business model, but you develop a high retention rate, you can and will achieve a form of growing ARR in a way that mirrors the SaaS growth curve. While you add new customers, you retain existing customers; and because they are carefully vetted, healthy companies, they survive and also grow while they are with you. So, the revenues stack and grow year over year with a degree of predictability usually seen only in SaaS or subscription-based businesses. Moreover, larger clients often need less handholding because their businesses are more mature and their personnel are more knowledgeable.

You see, this is the *real* story of your company's transformation. You have to find the right kind of customer. This is a lot easier when you're starting with a blank slate, but that's probably not what you're dealing with unless you're a brand-new company. Chances are, you have at least a fledgling business going, so you're already reaching out to some target customers and have some customer base in place.

It's entirely possible that one of your biggest problems is that you're going after the wrong targets. How can you determine when your current approach isn't working—and, just as importantly, how can you pivot to a better target? This is probably going to be the single most impactful part of the entire process we outline in this book. Somehow, you have to figure out who your ideal customer is, then align every part of your business toward that target. This is commonly known as the Ideal Customer Profile (ICP), but simply defining your ICP isn't enough.

It's also not enough to simply point your salespeople at the right audience. Somehow, you have to align every single person on every team within your organization around your ideal customer. Your current and future products and services, your SEO, paid marketing, social media, PR, messaging, geographic locations, partnerships, and more need to be fully aligned to your target, not just your sales team. Even your mission statement might change.

Everything in the company has to turn in the new direction with *discipline*. In my experience, for companies to succeed, this is the single most impactful decision they will make toward achieving phenomenal growth. Many are going after everyone and everything, aiming at every possible target, and for all of their hard work, they are not pulling in nearly enough revenue per year for every customer. At the same time, many have enormous churn, because many of their customers are very small companies who are dying on the vine. They are each doing very little business. They have a very small margin of error and frequently just fall off the map.

If you want to grow, you simply have to shift your attention toward the right customers, and that often means larger ones. Now, it's important to realize that just because you shift your target doesn't mean you can change everything all at once, especially in the B2B world. Indeed, it will likely mean that you have to ratchet up to bigger customers over time, though I have seen that when moving fast, near-immediate progress is possible.

As you ratchet up to bigger customers, you push your ceiling higher and higher. Larger contracts may give you more "bang for your buck." They also churn a lot more slowly, because big companies tend to survive and thrive into the future and make decisions much more slowly. Also, because they make changes far more slowly, I have found that if they are seeking to make a change because of a perceived gap in services or problem they are experiencing, with larger clients, this longer period required for them to make a change affords more time to address and resolve those issues or develop services that can fill the gap they are sensing. Ultimately this can, in fact, result in retaining the customer. Also, larger companies need far less handholding than the smaller ones do. I have found that smaller, less stable customers often need someone to teach them how to do business. You would likely be spending more time for less money, and with far less stable customers. When you ratchet up to bigger companies, however, you work less for more money and a more stable customer lifetime duration. From every standpoint—revenue to profitability to retention—it is often the best possible decision.

Again, this isn't just about sales. Marketing to small companies is far more expensive than marketing to large companies. Some business owners view their organizations as part-time interests, side gigs that they do at night and on weekends, so it is almost like trying to reach hobbyists or consumers. Many of them work out of their basements and garages. In order to scale, you would practically have to do consumer marketing, which is notoriously costly. Indeed, marketing to them is haphazard and expensive, and the results are often disappointing.

When you shift to larger customers, you will find that you are able to do a lot more with far fewer marketing dollars. It might seem counterintuitive. Shouldn't it cost more to reach a bigger company? I have found just the opposite to be true.

Doing this type of analysis—looking at your current customer mix; what it is or isn't bringing you; what it's costing you in terms of time, money, and focus; looking at it in terms of customer lifetime duration and value; and including churn factors that are inherent in the customer profile—is critical. You may find, as I have over and over again, that customer size matters. In your case, you may want to go for smaller rather than larger customers. But you may find other factors, too, such as what they consume and how, whether there is inherent seasonality, and what their geographical needs are. Really look at whether your current customer base serves you ideally and craft a real Ideal Customer Profile that solves for and backs into your actual goals.

ICP AND QUALIFIER

For all of these reasons and more, you may well have to pivot. Even though you aren't moving to a different line of business, you may have to change almost everything about your approach in order to align your entire organization with your new target customer. In my experiences over the years, I have had to change the way we sold, how and where we marketed, the way we interacted with prospective customers, what partnerships we wanted to pursue, and how we wanted to pursue them. It was not easy. However, once we implemented our ICP cross-functionally in a disciplined way, the end result was that we began to grow by leaps and bounds.

While ratcheting up the average size of your ideal customer, the leaps will get bigger, and your approach will have to change a little bit more with each ratchet. With larger customers, you may have to develop different types of relationships, and you may have to implement ever more sophisticated products, services, integrations, and capabilities that you hadn't needed to before.

You will also have to develop new capabilities for customer service and success for the post-sale period, and that means training the people who manage the larger accounts to service through longer periods of time and sharper growth. On the sales side, you will have to change your thinking about who your ideal customer is in a more complex and nuanced way in order to deal with larger and more complex customers.

An Ideal Customer Profile is a good starting point, but because it's an ideal, it is not fully actionable. You need a practical tool that can act as a yardstick for benchmarking opportunities. Unlike the ideal, the real world is filled with complexity, ranges, and nuance. For that reason, once you understand your ICP, it's important to create an actual qualifier that sales and marketing can use, against which they can gauge leads and opportunities. The qualifier is a grid-form tool that defines a number of qualifying factors, as well as several qualification statuses that relate to those factors. And because there will always be exceptions, you can list the most common of those as a go-with to the qualifier. Table 1 is an example of a useful structure.

This doesn't have to be fully rigid. You can formalize a list of common exceptions. An exceptions list is useful because then sales and marketing people can make judgment calls on the fly and only go to upper management on matters that are true "exception handling" of an unusual sort.

Table 1.

Qualifying Factors	Not Qualified	Possibly Qualified	Fully Qualified	Ideal

By providing them with a qualifier aimed at new target customers, along with a standardized set of exceptions, you can give your sales and marketing people the ability to make judicious use of the scorecard, and upper management only has to handle extreme exceptions that are not on the standardized exception list. With that formalized list of exceptions, it's possible to give your salespeople what feels like a laissez-faire approach to make their best judgments when potential customers don't otherwise meet the qualifiers. This is important, because sometimes a really great opportunity might not seem to meet the qualification criteria at first glance, but you don't want to miss out on it.

It's important to point out that this kind of migration is not easy. Saying no to money is a hard thing to do. There may be some small business customers that appear good on the surface, and certainly appear healthy at certain points in time, but there is no way to know how they will develop in the future. You have to draw a line somewhere and create self-definition. At scale and on average, some types of customers are not good for you, and you simply have to bite the bullet and act on your knowledge and convictions. It requires a form of courage to do so, and to accept that you cannot be all things to all people.

Just because you won't work with a certain customer now doesn't mean you will never work with them in the future, so make sure to treat everyone well. I have always made sure that, even when we turn some customers down, we make sure to point them in the direction of other potential companies who are better suited for their size and needs. And we remind them that when they outgrow those providers, we will be ready, willing, and able to provide the services they need.

In your case, a customer might be too big now, but someday they may have a smaller division you want to work with. Or you may have a customer whose geography is currently undesirable but may change in the future. So remember: just because a company doesn't fit your ICP or qualifier today doesn't mean you won't work with them tomorrow.

You will find that some of the same businesses come back to you, but you will get them back when they are later in their life cycles and when they have grown beyond their more dangerously risky and unstable early phases. Instead of taking them on when they are still in their infancy, you will take them at a higher level of maturity. In a strange way, it is almost like being an investor. You have to decide how much risk you are willing to take on when investing your limited time and resources with customers.

And what will the end result be? When you do a cohort analysis it will become quite clear.

The bigger customers that you take on later will have much higher retention and growth rates because you looked at their viability signals through the use of your qualifier scorecard. Indeed, with your new qualifiers, your retention and growth rates will skyrocket, and churn will plummet. Remember, a mere 5 percent increase in retention leads to a 25 to 95 percent increase in revenue, so you can see how a much higher retention contributes directly to exponential growth.

THE MOST VALUABLE THING YOU CAN DO

Indeed, retention is the most valuable thing you can do for your company. Nothing compares. If you have to spend your time, money, and energy on one specific business aspect, let it be retention. Find the *right* customers, the ones who are more likely to be able to stick around and grow, the ones who are more profitable for you and require the least handholding, and then *keep them*.

I have seen companies who have raised hundreds of millions of dollars and hired dozens of salespeople but were not generating nearly enough revenue. This was because their business was a revolving door. They were bringing in the wrong customers, unstable small businesses who were quick to jump ship or actually go under, and they needed a standing army of salespeople in order to refill their leaky churn bucket. That is never going to be a recipe for long-term viability. They burned through hundreds of millions of dollars building an unprofitable business because they constantly needed to bring in new customers to offset the customers who left.

Create a pattern of net revenue retention during the pre-sale process by choosing the right customers. If you do that, you will give yourself the highest possible chance for retention, and it's a strategic move that costs you nothing. In fact, it's little more than a thought experiment carried through to action across your entire organization.

Which ideal customer is most likely to stick around and require the least handholding? Identify that target and aim everything toward them. Set your new qualifiers and pivot, even if you have to adjust gradually in order to get everyone aligned. That's how you create stackable revenue and dramatic business growth.

And how do you reach that ideal customer? Selling alone isn't enough. You need to be providing them value long before they ever speak to your sales team. To do that, we recommend becoming thought leaders in your industry.

Exercises to Build Your Playbook

- Clearly identify your ICP—your Ideal Customer Profile.

  _____

  _____

  _____

- Now craft a qualifier. What are the qualification criteria? How
  do you define unqualified, potentially qualified, and ideal?
  Complete this qualifier template for your own business:

  _____

  _____

  _____

Qualifying Factors	Not Qualified	Possibly Qualified	Fully Qualified	Ideal

- What in your organization do you need to align toward your ideal customer?

  _____

  _____

  _____

- What will the process be to qualify and disqualify, and how will you communicate disqualification to the prospects?

  _____

  _____

  _____

- What would be your standardized list of exceptions?

  _____

  _____

  _____

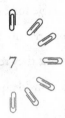

7

Thought Leadership

"Share your knowledge. It is a way to achieve immortality."

—THE DALAI LAMA

WHEN YOU MAKE A DECISION TO PRESERVE capital and equity, you necessarily decide to think differently about marketing. In the case of my over-funded competitor (and other examples that abound today), it's clear that many companies blindly spend their VC raises on digital marketing, forking over millions of dollars to Google, Facebook, and LinkedIn. If you've decided to do otherwise, then necessity is the mother of invention. That means you have to find creative ways to get out there into the world while also differentiating yourself, and you have to do it in a way that will cost you little or practically nothing.

This is a common struggle for early phase and small businesses. They have a very limited marketing budget, but somehow, they still have to market themselves if they're going to survive. Ask yourself the most obvious and reasonable question: "What marketing can we do that's totally free?"

As it turns out, there are a few options. One marketing approach you can use that is highly effective and costs you nothing is *thought leadership*.

SHARING CONTENT FOR FREE

Earlier, we talked about the importance of positioning yourself at the center of your industry, and this is the tactic where that mindset comes into play. You make yourself the center of your industry by positioning yourself as a thought leader who provides regular value through shared content, and you do it without spending a dime.

Again, you're not standing up and crowning yourself emperor. It's not like some kid standing up in the middle of a classroom and announcing, "By the way, everyone, I'm the smartest kid in the room. I just wanted you all to know that."

Rather, this is about being radically generous with thought leadership through articles, conferences, webinars, infographics, and other content, as well as one-to-one communication. You don't need a PhD in a subject to share expertise and ideas about it. Your company doesn't have to be in an industry for a hundred years before you dare to speak from a position of experience.

A child who has just learned their ABCs can turn around and teach a younger child their ABCs. They don't have to earn their teaching license first. The same idea is at work here. Even if you're a young business, still in your infancy or your early days in an industry, you possess some kind of knowledge or experience that is of value to other businesses and that you can share generously with others.

Combine this generous sharing of experience and wisdom with the mindset goal of making yourself the center of your industry, and you create a powerful platform for the exchange of ideas and content. And you can do this with absolutely no budget. For example, anyone can write and publish a LinkedIn article. It doesn't cost anything to sign up, create your profile, and begin creating articles.

Where you lack knowledge, you can invite other companies and business leaders to participate with you for shared and mutual benefit. Not only can you begin posting articles on topics related to your work, expertise, experiences, and industry, but you can leverage partnerships with other companies and publish through shared platforms.

Partnership-based content leverages the aggregate wisdom of all of your partner companies and gives you tons of meaningful content to share—and, as it turns out, other businesses have a strong desire to get their own brands out there into the world. Many of them will gladly work with you in order to gain a bit more exposure.

Of course, to create thought leadership content, you need some people who have the bandwidth to sit down and write. Eventually, you can hire a part- or full-time contractor or employee to create content, but for at least a while, everything may be written by you or someone on your current team. This can then be supplemented with content from a wide range of industry experts, some from partner companies and some not.

You will discover that people love to be invited to write and publish things, so don't be afraid to ask someone for an interview, a few quotes, or a piece of thought leadership. Leverage customers, partners, and other people in your industry to create content with you—just make sure you're the one doing the publishing. Encourage them to do so, as well. This way, you will multiply your audience.

You need to be involved in some way with every piece of content being created. The genesis of the content comes from you, and they are writing for you. You will potentially grow a bench of hundreds of people you could call on at any time to write for you and with you.

Beyond writing articles, you can also create events and invite partners to participate. Of course, an in-person event is going to cost some money, but virtual mini-conferences have become a perfectly viable option, especially in the post-COVID-19 era. You can create virtual mini-conferences, bringing both partners and customers together to talk about a variety of topics.

These kinds of events can take many different forms, from one-on-one interviews to panel discussions. They can be onsite, even with very little budget. This type of event series can differentiate you tremendously from your competitors because it is likely that no one else in your industry is doing it. Once you get the ball rolling on a hub or platform for sharing content, it's hard for other organizations to catch up. Indeed, you can create an entire body of work before anyone else wakes up to the potential. By then, you can take what you've created and begin marketing it through social media.

Then you can create additional content that is gated, where people can only access it by signing up for your email list and possibly providing other information. This helps you grow your own house list, which you can market to with future content. It's a compounding growth pattern, constantly feeding itself and getting bigger over time. We found that sharing new content with an existing list can sometimes wake up dormant accounts, even as it reaches new people.

ONE-TO-ONE THOUGHT LEADERSHIP

Thought leadership doesn't have to be one to many; it can also take the form of one-to-one consultative help. Why would someone who is not yet your customer, and may not even *want* to become your customer at this point, approach you for an in-depth discussion? Because they're already familiar with you as a thought leader in the industry and through partnerships with other companies. Remember, you've positioned yourself at the center of your industry.

Since they already know you, your head of business development, VP of partnerships, or customer success team can meet with them to provide consultative advice (not just pitching a product or service). For example, maybe a business leader thinks they're going to need an ERP system within a year or two. Normally, they wouldn't discuss this with a company like yours—unless you had already created and shared so much meaningful content on this subject that they viewed it as an existing relationship. They would know you through your content, and you would have created an ecosystem of partnerships and alliances with other companies.

Consequently, plenty of people in the industry who aren't your customers will know that they can come to you with questions anytime they need to. You will then get to have broader conversations with them. In doing this, even if you are not directly making a sale, you will be continuing to plant yourselves in people's minds as their go-to resource. You'll already be establishing yourselves as thought leaders through articles, events, podcasts, and so on, and you'll be deepening those relationships through one-on-one consultative conversations.

TAKING IT TO THE NEXT LEVEL

Eventually, creating content for your own platforms—including your company's LinkedIn page and other social media platforms—will lead to writing articles for publications like *Forbes* and *Fast Company*. Some of those articles will help you win awards. There are a number of award applications that are either free or cheap, and when you apply, they generally ask you for other things you've done. This enables you to link your award to additional content you've created, which leads to even more views and interactions.

All of this thought leadership, which costs you very little, will wind up laying a far more solid groundwork for phenomenal growth than if you had spent tens of thousands of dollars on PR or millions on paid search. Moreover, once you're known to publications as a thought leader, they will begin coming to you and asking for more. You become an easy resource for them, just as they continue to be a resource for you.

You might expect it to take a long time to build up a reputation as a thought leader, but it doesn't have to. You can make enormous strides in developing an award-winning body of work and becoming a known thought leader in your industry within six months to a year. Cultivate specific people within your organization to become voices in the industry and start putting content out there.

Once you have a nice body of work, you can take it to the next level by creating your own platform or space around your thought leadership. This might be a virtual space that you create and manage where the free flow of ideas can happen. It might be an ongoing event series, an online educational platform like an online "academy" or "university," or more.

In other words, take what you're already doing, your thought leadership content, and put a wrapper around it. Turn it into a platform and develop a membership base that you invite, and allow people to participate *free of cost*, whether or not they're customers or partners. It's almost like a trade association, but it's not monetized.

Most trade associations charge people on both sides—the members, and the sponsors who sell to those members. Of the two, sponsors bear the greater costs for running the association; but in return, they get to set up booths at trade shows and try to sell to the member companies in their industry. You've no doubt attended these kinds of trade shows before. They have a very strong "hunter and hunted" mentality, as sponsors in the booths try desperately to have conversations with the members walking the trade show floor.

Since people are paying to be part of these trade associations, there's a financial incentive to make them worth doing. But when you don't monetize your trade association, you create a space for more open conversations where you can relax and spend real quality time with customers, prospects, and partners. Nobody has an ax to grind. Everyone is there to better the industry, and as a result, really good things can happen.

Beyond publishing content, think about what kind of platform, association, or event series you can create and invite others to participate in. You're not monetizing this; you're simply inviting people to participate. That's radical generosity at work in conjunction with thought leadership, and it transforms you into a magnanimous "giver of opportunity" in your industry and beyond. All of the thought leadership you gather gets connected to you because it's centered around your event.

The impact of this on your company will be even more than you anticipate. You will spend a little on management of events and activities, and occasionally, a little on content development—a press release here and there—but otherwise, all this thought leadership is cost-free.

ALWAYS BE IN THE ROOM

How does all of this translate into revenue? The simple answer is that you are extending your funnel on the front end. How do you normally fill the top of your sales funnel? The best way is through inbound marketing, the highest-intent marketing there is, because the people who come to you are already searching for what you have to offer. They're knocking on *your* door because they want what you're selling.

Businesses tend to focus on outbound marketing, where salespeople work hard to bring in new customers, because something about salespeople's efforts feels appealing—but, in fact, this is the lowest-intent marketing. You're knocking on *their* door, hoping they'll open up and let you in. But they might not need what you have, or they might need it but not *right now*. Even with good leads, it's hard to meet prospects at the exact right moment, so your salespeople wind up "dialing for dollars."

What if you happened to be in the room with someone the moment their need came up? Isn't that the dream? That's the ideal scenario, after all. Don't you just wish a little birdie would fly through your window and whisper in your ear, "So-and-so has a need today." That would make things so much easier.

The only way to achieve something comparable is to make sure you're present as much as possible when needs arise—so that you are always in the room. No matter how many salespeople you hire, or how many calls they make, you're never going to be right there in a prospect's room the second they realize they have a need. Statistically speaking, this just doesn't happen. However, you can create an environment where you're always part of the conversation—where you've become the natural go-to for information and answers, and you are always in the room.

In a sense, you're creating a conceptual room where everyone is hanging out, listening and learning, talking to each other, and opening up far more opportunities to see those needs arise and meet them at the right moment. Moreover, you own and operate the room—it is your room. This is what I mean by extending your sales funnel on the front end. Indeed, the front end of the funnel is going to become much, much larger. When you've been providing value for a long time, people are going to naturally come to you because they already know you have answers. You will also be there to sense when the soft demand signals arise. You're creating an environment where you can stay softly in the picture for prospects, so you'll be there far more often at the right time for the right people. This is the antechamber to your funnel.

If you create a platform or a forum, does all of it have to be free? Not necessarily. You might have some services that are reserved only for people who become paying customers, but you will have a tremendous response from pushing almost everything into a free model.

Of course, getting other companies to participate in your own thought leadership requires making it mutually beneficial. Create partnerships with numerous companies in your industry who are not your direct competitors and see how very far they can take you. Let's look at how you can do that.

Exercises to Build Your Playbook

- What kind of regular thought leadership content can you provide on free platforms like LinkedIn or your own website?

  _____

  _____

  _____

- What current or prospective partner companies can you invite to contribute to your thought leadership platform?

  _____

  _____

  _____

- What kind of consultative help can you provide to companies who are not yet your customers?

  _____

  _____

  _____

- What platform, association, or event series can you create and invite others to participate in (without monetizing it)?

_____

_____

_____

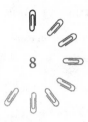

8

Develop Partnerships

"We are caught in an inescapable network of
mutuality, tied in a single garment of destiny."
—DR. MARTIN LUTHER KING, JR.

A COMPANY THAT CREATES A SHARP FOCUS ON
partnerships often finds that a large portion of their revenues come directly from partnerships as a lead source.
First of all, let's break down what I mean when I say *partnerships*.
Typically, a partner is a company that is adjacent to, but—with
some notable exceptions—not competitive with your company,
and that agrees to work with you in some capacity in order to

share resources and referrals for mutual benefit. Bear in mind, the closer a partner is to the actual nature of your products or services, the better.

Many companies have a partner page on their website that shows a list of company logos from businesses that supposedly have some kind of relationship with them. However, the vast majority of the time, the partners listed there have never actually delivered the company a penny in revenue. There are many reasons for this. When you're talking about very large enterprises, they usually have partnership structures that are very rigid. However, this is almost never the case with a very small company, for whom any partnership might be far less sharply defined and unclear. Avoid having these vanity logos. Instead, create real living partnerships that represent revenue streams for all concerned.

So, the big questions are: How do you find companies to partner with? Why would anyone want to partner with a small company in the first place? What can a small company possibly offer in return? As we said, anyone who is selling into the same industry as you is a potential partner. Some partners and partnerships can be tightly coupled and might even integrate with you directly. For example, an order management company with an e-commerce platform might integrate directly with your company's API for returns management or international shipping. In that case, data would flow in both directions and there would be both technology/product and business aspects to the partnership.

A partnership doesn't have to work this way. Indeed, there are various degrees of relevance that a partner might have with you. It might just be two B2C companies who aren't direct competitors that sell to the same target base, or it might be two B2B businesses that sell to the same people within their target companies. To use my company as an example, a marketing technology company might sell to the same business in our industry, but they target the project management department, while we sell to the head of operations or the CFO. Maybe we sell to the same people, but they sell at a different time or for a different need—or both.

When a customer expresses a need, you can often infer they are also experiencing other types of needs at the same time. It is a growth signal that they have outgrown their old provider, and they are probably outgrowing other things, as well. Therefore, you could partner with other companies providing those other products and services alongside your own.

Generally, you can partner with companies who are the same size as you, or have roughly the same number of customers, though it's great to "marry up" to partners who could handle many more customers than you could. They typically also have much broader marketing than you would.

But why would larger companies like these want to work with a smaller partner like you? Why would a much larger company with broader marketing, such as Microsoft, see any value in such a professional partnership? There are a few reasons. Firstly, you may be giving them quick time to market on product completion. In other words, your solution is something they do not provide but their customers want. By partnering, you may be providing them completion of their solution that they can offer their customers. Secondly, you may have a swath of customers they covet but do not yet have. Don't sell yourself short. If they want to partner with you, it is because you bring something of real value to them.

You will introduce customers to them, and they will introduce customers to you. That's the basic idea behind partnership, though it occurs in many different forms. You can mutually monetize through revenue share or royalties for this exchange of leads, but you don't have to. For example, there might be a royalty scheme that requires a certain percentage of revenue be paid for each customer you give to a partner company in the first year or two.

In the best partnerships, and also in partnerships when you truly are marrying up, partnering with a larger company like NetSuite or Microsoft, that partner doesn't care much about the 2 or 3 percent a small company pays them for a customer referral. They simply are not interested in that payment, so why would they partner in the first place? What are they in it for?

To sell more of their own products and services. As noted, the number one reason is that a small company may fill a gap for them, offering something that they don't have and do not necessarily want to build or buy themselves. By allowing another business to fill that gap, they can sell more of what they're already selling. Your offering is complementary to their own, filling in a gap that their offering lacks, which keeps customers from shopping for a more complete solution elsewhere.

In fact, you may be surprised by the companies that will say yes to such an arrangement. We've seen many David-and-Goliath partnerships between very large companies and very small ones, and Goliath isn't in it for the royalty checks but rather for the referrals—as well as for the completeness that comes from complementary offerings. Indeed, these kinds of partnerships tend to work very well.

The point is, you don't have to be a giant business in order to provide critical value to a partnership, even when it is with a very large company. Even the smallest of companies can fill a gap in a way that is mutually beneficial.

GIVE MORE THAN YOU RECEIVE

The most important element for managing partnerships is a tactical approach rooted in a mindset that we've already talked about: radical generosity. Always give much, much more than you're getting. Understandably, people are often concerned about whether they are getting enough as part of a fair and equitable two-way relationship. "We gave them *this* many leads, but they only gave us *that* many." While it might seem counterintuitive, the approach that I've found to be most effective is to hyper-focus on giving far more to your partners than they give to you.

Any time a partner gives a customer referral, make sure to give them several referrals in return. This not only grows the relationship, but it also makes it easier to throttle your partnerships when needed. If you needed twenty new leads tomorrow, you could contact partners, and the perceived "outstanding credit" that you have with them would make it far more likely that you'd get those leads. "They've been so generous to us; how can we possibly refuse?" That is the thinking. In fact, they will be rather excited to pay you back in kind for your ongoing generosity.

If you keep up a discipline of constantly giving more than you receive in times when you have no acute need, then when your time of acute need arises, you can throttle it at a moment's notice. Just pick up the phone and start contacting those grateful partners. The relationship is already levered in your favor.

To maintain this, you have to be careful about replenishing your supply of good will, keeping yourself in a position of giving more than receiving at all times. Not only can you throttle this for new leads, but those leads will be much warmer, pre-qualified, and further down the funnel than anything you'd get from a Google ad.

Of course, you have to take special care of those partnership leads, because you don't want to kill the goose that lays the golden eggs. If you mess up an account from a standard lead source, the potential cost is only that one account. But if you fumble an account whose lead source is a partner, you put an entire lead source at risk. Partnership leads and accounts must be treated with special care at all times, and ways to make sure that everyone in the organization has a sensitivity to the source of these leads and accounts must be put in place.

WHO SHOULD YOUR PARTNERS BE?

By and large, your best partners are going to be companies that are non-competitive and adjacent to you—those who sell into your target industry, and preferably also sell into the same roles and personas within target companies as you. It is also possible to partner with an actual competitor and become, as they say, "frenemies." These are companies whose Ideal Customer Profile overlaps with yours—but not entirely. In those cases, you will have certain leads that you compete for, and obviously you can't share them. However, there are other categories of accounts that you *don't* compete for, and they are fair game for sharing within the context of partnership.

For example, if you are an e-commerce fulfillment company, there are probably certain aspects of the business you do not cover (e.g., refrigerated or frozen items, large bulky things, or perhaps apparel that requires highly specific cleaning and mold remediation). Fortunately, there are other companies out there who love to do what you don't do. Yes, there may be some things you will compete on, but if they get a lead that's outside of their scope, they have nothing to lose and everything to gain by sharing it with you.

There is usually no lack of leads to share with competitive partners. In digital marketing, most leads that come into an organization are unqualified, so they get tossed out. However, you can now pass those leads along to a "frenemy" organization. Keep a running list of your competitors and their Ideal Customer Profiles, with an eye on how they differ from your own. That way, as leads come in, you can quickly find a destination for an unqualified lead instead of simply discarding it. Every company deals with what one of the best partnership executives I know likes to call "inverse qualified leads," which refers to leads that aren't a good fit for you but *are* a good fit for a company adjacent to you, or vice versa. These leads are your relationship currency with partners.

With many partners, I have had formal agreements; but that's not always the case. Sometimes, with frenemies, not only will you *not* have a formal agreement, but you may not even speak to each other. You may simply get leads who tell you they were sent over by your frenemy. Don't wait for that to happen, though. Start sending them yourself, and make sure the lead lets your partner know that you did the sending. You may eventually get a call from a partner wanting to discuss a more formal arrangement, or you might just start getting leads. Either way, it's beautiful and effortless.

In my experience, you can develop so many frenemy lead sources that they make up a large proportion of your total partnership leads. In some instances, this happens almost in secret, like students passing notes under their desks in a classroom. You're both doing it, and you know you're doing it, but you don't publicly acknowledge it because you are, after all, technically competing with each other where your ICPs do overlap.

Ideally, your partnerships will become a huge driver of your thought leadership, as you invite partners of all kinds to participate in platforms and events, including advisory councils, thought leadership and networking events, webinars, content production, and much more. This partnership approach is all the more effective when you adopt a solution-selling approach to your business. We'll examine what that means next.

Exercises to Build Your Playbook

- Make a list of categories of companies that are adjacent to but
  not competitive with you who sell into your Ideal Customer
  Profile.

  _____

  _____

  _____

  _____

- Populate each category with specific company names and
  highlight or asterisk those who sell into the same role or
  persona within your targets, as they are extra valuable.
  - Knowing what you do about your current customers
    and recent leads, who could benefit from the goods and
    services of these partners?

    _____

    _____

    _____

    _____

- Make a list of frenemies: those companies who compete with you on some but not all business. These are the companies whose ICPs only partially overlap with yours.

  _____

  _____

  _____

  _____

- Do a retrospective of the last three months of inbound leads that have come in. Of the ones that are disqualified for your ICP, highlight those which may be qualified for your frenemy partners.

  _____

  _____

  _____

  _____

9

A Solution-Selling Approach

*"People don't want to buy a quarter-inch
drill. They want a quarter-inch hole!"*
—THEODORE LEVITT

YOU'RE PROBABLY ALREADY FAMILIAR WITH THE
terms *marketing qualified leads* and *sales qualified leads*—
but what if you could apply what in the consumer SaaS
space are typically thought of as *product qualified leads* to all arenas,
including enterprise B2B?

First, let's get our definitions straight:

- A **marketing qualified lead** is a prospect who expresses interest based on marketing efforts.
- A **sales qualified lead** is a prospect who has been vetted by your marketing team and is ready to talk to your sales team.
- A **product qualified lead** is a prospect who has already used a free version of your product.

For a common example of a product qualified lead, consider the case of Zoom. You can download and use the video conferencing product for free with certain restrictions. For example, calls have a forty-minute time limit, and you can only host up to one hundred participants. As soon as you decide you need longer calls, or more participants, or if you need to record your calls, then you hit a paywall. Suddenly, the free version of the software is no longer enough, and you need to transition to a paid version in order to continue meeting your needs.

How does this third category make any sense in a non-consumer arena like B2B, enterprise, and services? And how does it relate to consultative selling? The secret is in adapting what is typically thought of as a "freemium" business model concept to these arenas. With a freemium model, you offer customers a basic or limited version of your product or service and then charge them for more advanced features. The customers who become attached to the product through this version are product qualified leads for conversion to the paid version.

Did you know that the freemium model is the holy grail of revenue growth? In our experience, freemium models tend to grow quickly, are often viral, and have stackable revenue. A person using the free version is considered a *product qualified lead* because they're already demonstrating a fondness for the product by using it.

As a product qualified lead, it's easy to send them an email which says something like, "We love that you're using our product twelve times a day, but did you know there are dozens of other features you could be enjoying, as well?" You're giving away a piece of your product for free to see which users demonstrate an affinity for it.

You can do a similar thing with any product or service, even if it is not SaaS—but instead of giving away a limited version of a piece of software for free, you're giving away some time or knowledge for free. Instead of free product usage, the offer is: "I'd be happy to share some information with you right now," or "I'd like to understand your broader problems because I may be able to point you in the right direction."

The promise, spoken or unspoken, is: "If you were a customer, we'd be able to help you in so many more additional ways, but for now, here is some free information. I'd love to talk to you for a little while." Rarely do companies consider creating freemium models outside of software products, but in reality, that's exactly what a deeply consultative sales process is. It's an incredibly powerful way to use your own knowledge or expertise to create what are analogous to product qualified leads, where the product—among other things—is your relationship.

A CONSULTATIVE RELATIONSHIP

This is simply one more approach to being radically generous and non-transactional, and it goes hand-in-hand with what we call "solution selling." With solution selling, you are strategically positioning your products and services as a suite of answers that are specifically tailored to a customer's needs. Doing this *well* requires many of the mindsets and tactics we've already discussed.

First, it requires placing yourself at the center of your industry. Second, it requires a non-transactional approach. Third, it goes right along with being a thought leader.

A solution-selling approach turns the sales arc into a cycle that keeps feeding itself, because it's no longer an approach that has a dead end once you've made a transaction. Instead of simply trying to push a customer toward a sale, you are taking a consultative approach at every stage of the customer journey, having deep conversations and asking a lot of questions about their entire business.

Rather than running to get your pricing sheet, you're looking at everything they need, whether or not your company provides it, and discussing a full range of solutions with them to meet their every need. Remember, you should now have a wide array of partner companies who can provide solutions that you don't offer.

Put another way, you're getting right into the middle of their business lives to present real solutions, and importantly, using the word "solution" to describe products and services (because verbiage matters). Once you've discussed their needs, you're putting together a suite of options that potentially includes a range of products and services, and while pricing must be included in the solution you present, it is not the core. Remember, you're including your own products and services potentially *alongside* the products and services of partner companies.

Instead of, "Here are the products we offer, and here are the prices," you're saying, "We recommend the following solutions for your needs. Here's why we recommend them, how they will meet your needs, and what they would cost." In a transactional approach, that pricing sheet becomes the center of everything you're moving toward, and when you do that, it becomes a race to the bottom. You turn yourself into a commodity and install a dead end into your customer journey.

But a relationship with a trusted advisor never ends. When you have a relationship with a prospective customer that begins long before they ever approach you (because you're a thought leader who provides value to the industry) and continues long after (because you're *still* a thought leader providing value), then the sale of a product or service becomes merely one important step along the path of helping them—it's a natural outcome. You provide solutions, not products—and those solutions take the form of your thought leadership articles and events; your partnerships with other companies; your consultative conversations; and, yes, your products and services, as well.

Transitioning to this radically different approach has a huge impact on results. In the beginning, you were simply working toward transactions. Prospective customers would tell you what they needed, and you would likely send a pricing sheet.

"Oh, you need to get your products from here to there? Here's how much we would charge for it."

Then you would wait until you heard back from them. When you were working on a large deal, you might also have called them to review the pricing structure, but the pricing would have stood at the very heart of everything you did.

"Here's what we charge for what we do. Will you pay for it? Yes or no?"

Changing your whole approach to be consultative and non-transactional will be transformational. Instead of a pricing sheet, you will invest in creating a beautiful solution book, similar to what major consulting companies provide, that contains an analysis of various customer problems and a range of solutions. Once this booklet exists as a template, it provides value to customers all on its own, and it means you don't need salespeople to spend time and energy creating original content all the time.

When salespeople speak with a prospective customer, you should provide them with a "kitchen sink" slide deck that gives an all-inclusive look at everything your company has to offer. Then, for each instance, all salespeople have to do is customize the deck by changing the name and logo to match the customer, remove a few things that are not applicable, and add a few elements that are specific to that customer. This can be thought of as a reductive approach, deleting what doesn't belong from the kitchen sink deck rather than crafting new content over and over again.

When a customer receives this type of slide deck, it looks like someone has spent hours customizing it for them, but they haven't. They receive a deck that includes specific slides addressing the process (and, yes, pricing) for their specific needs, and the salesperson has removed irrelevant slides for other needs, along with slides that do not apply to this customer.

Alongside an exploration of the solutions you could provide to customers in order to meet their specific needs, you should also include a list of partners relevant to those needs and recommend a few who have solutions that could be integrated. And you can offer to make direct warm introductions to relevant people within those partner companies. This may be difficult to implement initially, but it's possible that no one in your industry or segment is doing it at the moment, so it can become a huge differentiator. It also has the additional benefit of feeding right into those partnerships in a radically generous way that ends up paying you back down the road.

Even when there is a formal request for proposal (RFP) you have to follow to the letter, send this slide deck along with it. That way, you have followed the desired format but also provided additional value.

Find a way to position what you have to offer as part of a solution set that goes well beyond mere transactions. Create a well-designed slide deck or booklet you can present to customers and prospects as a presentation of multiple solutions, not simply a pricing sheet.

This approach is particularly effective because it gives people a chance to experience what it would be like to work with you on an ongoing basis, and it creates the B2B version of product qualified leads. It transforms you in the eyes of prospective customers from a company merely trying to make a sale into a consultative company that really and truly wants to help. Your company isn't too small to take a solution-selling approach as part of becoming thought leaders, and as we experienced, it will enable you to leverage customer relationships in a way that leads to phenomenal growth.

Exercises to Build Your Playbook

- How can you strategically present your products and services as a suite of solutions to meet a customer's many needs?

  _____

  _____

  _____

- How can you position those solutions as one vital part of an ongoing relationship that provides value through thought leadership throughout a circular, unending life cycle for every customer?

  _____

  _____

  _____

- Create a solution book, similar to what major consulting companies put out, that contains an analysis of various customer problems and a range of solutions.

  _____

  _____

  _____

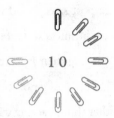

10

Leveraging Customer Relationships

"The fundamental law of human beings is interdependence.
A person is a person through other persons."
—ARCHBISHOP DESMOND TUTU

CUSTOMER REFERRAL IS THE STRONGEST REFER-ral you can get, because customers don't get anything out of it (e.g., no royalty payments). A partner referral is the second strongest, but there is at least some self-serving motive behind it, which makes it not entirely altruistic.

Since customer referrals are your strongest referrals, it's important to stay connected to customers at all times throughout their life cycle. The immediate post-sale period is especially important, because this is where repeat business and referrals take place. At this point, you're not just managing their interactions, but also deepening the relationship—a hallmark of a non-transactional approach.

This means, among other things, acting without knowing exactly what's going to come from it. This came rather easily to me because of my upbringing, but for many business leaders, it can seem counterintuitive or even counterproductive to do things for customers or prospects with no clear sense of what you're getting out of it.

There's just something about human nature that makes us forget to be thankful for things when we're already received them; in our minds, we're already chasing after the next thing that we want. We stay close to the prospect in the pre-sale and sort of exhale after the deal is done. Continuing to stay close to them post-signature, right after they buy but also immediately after and long into the future, can be a wonderful surprise to customers and a major differentiator.

The truth is, you don't know what else this one opportunity before you can bring unless you continue to have all kinds of discussions with customers after the sale. Create regular touchpoints with customers, and you can leverage those relationships in interesting ways before, during, and long after the sale. This can take many forms.

MINING THE POST-SALE RELATIONSHIP

When you mine the post-sale relationship, you accomplish a number of things. First of all, every customer hates to be treated without regard after they've been sold to. We've all experienced this as consumers at some point. We're wined and dined by sales until we finally close the deal, and then we're largely ignored or, at least, undervalued. Think about how easy it is to get hold of a salesperson when they're trying to convince you to buy from them, and how much harder it is to get hold of them after you sign.

When you work hard to maintain the post-sale relationship, it shows integrity—you're the same company before and after the sale—which demonstrates to customers that you're as good as your word. From there, you can leverage the post-sale relationship to create quarterly business reviews (QBRs), where you discuss with the customer how you did for them over the quarter and inform them of what's coming next for your company.

You can also offer a celebratory dinner for customers, especially if it's a large deal. You wined and dined them when they were prospects; now show them that they are just as important to you post-sale by wining and dining them again. This is a powerful gesture that shows them how much you continue to value the ongoing relationship, and customers receive it as an act of generosity.

"Wow, they didn't just want my money. They actually appreciate me! What a great company."

Sales doesn't have to disappear after the sale, either, even if they've turned that person over to a customer success team or customer support. The salesperson can stay in the picture, maintaining regular contact with them in some fashion. Again, this shows the customer that they are just as important as they were before the sale, and it demonstrates that they will continue to get the same amount of attention and service.

People are usually rather surprised when they get a follow-up call from the person who sold them a product or service. After all, people are enculturated to assume, "The salesperson got their commission. They're done with me." So, when you call them weeks or months later and invite them to a post-sales celebration of some kind, maybe a holiday party or cocktail hour, it's going to make a big impact. It demonstrates the value you place on the relationship. It also gives the customer another avenue to contact the company in case the customer success person isn't meeting their needs at some point.

This approach is especially important for larger customers, since they're typically going to be engaging with higher-order customer success assets in your company. For example, your largest customer might be directly involved with your VP of customer success on a regular basis, so if there's a problem that customer success fails to address properly, there's nowhere for the customer to escalate to.

However, if they have an ongoing relationship with their salesperson, then they at least have someone else they can vent to. Many customers don't want to complain about a problem directly to the person who is the source of it, so having additional contacts in the company that they feel comfortable with gives them other avenues. This is important because, sometimes, if a customer lacks another person to vent their problems to, they will slink away from your company rather than complain directly to the source of the problem.

Rather than waiting for customers to express their concerns of their own volition, you can also provide regular customer surveys. When you send surveys, give customers the option of identifying themselves or remaining anonymous, so they can be brutally honest.

REVIEWS, REFERRALS, AND REFERENCES

Consider the impact the post-sale relationship can have on your online reviews. We all get bad reviews from time to time. Even the greatest companies in the world get bad reviews. At one time, my company made an acquisition, and the transition went poorly on both sides. It wasn't anyone's fault, but the public perception laid the blame squarely in our laps. As a result, we received some bad reviews which we could do very little to address.

If you have a strong relationship with existing customers, you can find ways to counteract those bad reviews. Of course, you don't want to call customers up and say, "Hey, would you please give us a good review on the following review sites?" That's only going to direct happy customers to all of the bad reviews and possibly diminish their enthusiasm for your company.

However, there are some online services you can send customers to (e.g., Delighted) that will collect and distribute their positive reviews. With these kinds of services, you typically send out a very short survey that allows customers to provide a rating, with questions like, "Would you recommend this service to a friend?" If the rating is high enough, the customer is asked, "Would you be willing to write a review that we can publish?" If they agree and write a review, it is then published to all of the relevant business review websites, where it is verified and validated as real by the software. Importantly, these reviews go to the review websites *without* customers having to go there themselves.

You can also incentivize referrals, a tactic used by many companies to great effect. This can be as simple as saying, "We'll give you a $100 Amazon gift card for every lead you send us." Whatever reward you choose to give, make sure the customer can get it right away, as soon as you prove it's a qualified lead. Of course, before you set up an incentive program, you need to discuss it with your HR or legal department to make sure everything is kosher. Customers have to be reminded that the money they receive is taxable income, so that will need to go in the fine print somewhere.

This kind of incentive can be gamified in a fun way through a referral program, and it can also be extended to both customers and partners. Some companies have very specific restrictions about anything related to actual money. If that's the case, you might make a charitable contribution for the customer instead of sending them cash directly. Fortunately, there are many ways to approach this, so make sure your incentive program works for you, your sales team, and your customers.

Beyond customer *referrals*, there are also customer *references*. Sometimes, before a prospective customer will sign on the dotted line, they want to talk to a couple of references who are happy with your products and services. For example, my teams have occasionally received calls asking for references from existing customers. At this point, it is key that your sales team connect with your customer service and/or account management teams to understand the customer's current sentiment.

Ask them, "Is Acme Corporation happy with your services? Can we ask them about it?" Customer sentiment can swing wildly from day to day or even moment to moment. Even your most devoted and loyal customers may have difficult moments over the years, so you need to make sure your request for a referral not only comes from the right customer, but also takes place at the right time.

To address this, you can create a user-defined field in Salesforce or whatever CRM you use for "current customer sentiment." That way, salespeople, customer success, and account management can see at a glance which customers had a high positive sentiment at any given time and those who are currently experiencing issues. From there, they can identify specific customers relevant to a prospect that they could call and request a reference from. When this is implemented with fidelity, it saves tons of time and energy for the referral process.

It's also a smart idea to bring delighted existing customers together with your prospective customer. Create events where they can mix and mingle in a room, and let your delighted customers do the direct selling for you. They will evangelize your company in the most credible way possible. Customers who have a strong relationship with you and a very positive sentiment toward your company are going to promote and persuade prospects in ways salespeople never could.

Companies often rely on testimonials, whether written or on video, but you can also explore co-publishing with customers.

This could be a white paper, an infographic, or an article. These formats eliminate some of the awkwardness of testimonials—and, unlike testimonials, a co-published article is hard to remove from the public domain once published. Plus, it's a lot less awkward to co-contribute to an article or white paper than it is to ask a customer to praise your company in a testimonial. With that said, the implied testimonial is always there, and sometimes overt testimonial comments end up in the pieces as part of the natural course of content development.

INVEST IN RETAINING RELATIONSHIPS

Leveraging customer relationships effectively requires a deep foundation of trust, and trust can only be earned through actual experience over time. This makes retention very important. Remember, as we said, even a 5 percent increase in retention can lead to a 25 to 95 percent increase in revenue. If you're going to put your money toward anything, put it toward retention. Never skimp on anything you can do to retain a customer.

Even if your business isn't a SaaS company, you can create a growth ramp that *looks* very much like a SaaS company, scaling fast through retention simply because you don't have to constantly acquire and then re-acquire customers. When you lose customers, it's like a hole in a bucket of water that you're constantly trying to fill—it takes a lot of expense and hard work just to stay at the same level for less growth.

However, you can stop up that hole in two ways. First, as a preventative measure, you can choose the right customers. Second, you can retain those customers. A full bucket is a lot easier to keep filled than a bucket that constantly leaks, so this is well worth all of the time, attention, and money you throw at it.

So, what are the best ways to boost retention? As we said, the first thing you can do is to target customers who are more retainable. This varies from industry to industry, but in general, larger deals churn less often. For example, when we increased our average customer size, our retention increased dramatically, as well, and we found we struggled a lot less with renewals. It may be different in your situation, but this brings us back to creating your customer alignment, ICP, and a qualifier with a focus on LTV instead of just order value (i.e., which customers are likely to spend the most, partly as a result of being the most retainable).

Often, companies try to force retention by maintaining a stranglehold on their customers and creating an unspoken or overt threat to them over leaving. Chief among these are fees for terminating as well as making it very difficult to leave. This may slightly extend your customer relationship, but it's a hollow victory. It creates ill

will, harms your reputation, and precludes reigniting the relationship at a later time.

It's best to make sure that no customer has to pay through the
nose on the way out *ever*. It turns out, when you remove all of the
threats and penalties, retention improves. When customers can
leave anytime they want without being punished for it, they feel
better about you across the board. Break-up fees and penalties are
meant to be a deterrent, but they actually drive more people away
than they retain. Ultimately, people who want to leave will just take
the financial or convenience hit and leave anyway. The only difference is that they'll leave your company disliking you.

Their thought will be, "The company didn't meet my needs,
so I left, and they kicked me on the way out the door. I'll never
work with them again, and I won't send anyone their way!" How
is there *any advantage whatsoever* to instilling this attitude in former customers?

If you decide to continue being generous to customers on their
way out, to continue your non-transactional, consultative, rela-
tional approach even as they walk out the door and *beyond*, you will
gain immeasurably. As a result, you will begin getting great referrals
from people who have left you, and in many cases, those who leave
will wind up coming back. Maybe you didn't meet their needs at
the time, so they left. But because they continue to have a positive

feeling about you, once you are able to meet that need, they happily return without hesitation.

"You didn't offer service to Biloxi, so I left to find someone who did. But now that you've added Biloxi to your service areas, I'll happily return."

Difficult moments with customers are inevitable, but if you adopt the attitude that if someone leaves, it doesn't have to be the end of their involvement with your company, you will benefit. You will stay connected to them, even if indirectly, which means you can continue to mine that relationship in the future. I have been surprised by just how many great referrals have come from former customers, and how many customers return long after they've left.

To boost your retention rate, give people in your organization a generous enough budget that they are empowered to make customers happy in the moment. In most companies, people simply aren't authorized to spend at the customer success or account management level, but this is an area where you absolutely should not skimp. Within limits, give your people enough money and resources—and, just as importantly, the *authority*—to make customers happy without needing to get approval from anyone else first. This one decision alone can have a profound impact on your retention rate.

Earlier, we talked about having a mindset of staying ahead of customer needs, and that contributes greatly to retention, as well.

Many customers leave because they've outgrown their provider, or their needs have changed and are no longer being met. There are two ways to address this.

First, make sure every team member is thoroughly educated about everything your company can do. I've seen customers leave providers because they were told by an ill-informed team member that the provider didn't do something that they actually did.

Additionally, make sure your entire team is aware of what your company has on its near- and long-term roadmaps. Sometimes, a customer will leave because they foresee a future need you do not currently provide for. If this solution is already on your roadmap and your whole team knows about it and can articulate it well, the account can be saved. Share that you are, in fact, launching it soon, and that may be good enough for the wavering customer to stay with you.

Keep your finger on the pulse of what your customers might need in the future that you do not currently have on your roadmap. We talked about this in Chapter Four, but as a reminder, you do this through advisory councils, quarterly business reviews, surveys, ongoing conversations, and other touchpoints with customers during the post-sale relationship.

If you see a specific customer need developing, you may not have a solution right now; but if you can acknowledge your awareness of this future need, customers are more likely to hang in there with you. "We know this will be a problem for you in the future," you can say, "so we're developing a solution for it. We'll have it in six months."

USE YOUR RETENTION MECHANISMS

So, it turns out, you have many mechanisms at your disposal for boosting customer retention—which, in turn, will have a dramatic impact on your revenue growth. Mine the post-sale relationship to stay ahead of their needs. If you see a need on the horizon, create a plan for dealing with it and let your customers know about it.

Talk to your customers! Use quarterly business reviews and surveys to keep the lines of communication open. Invite customers to events. Request testimonials and co-published articles, white papers, and more. Be radically generous to your customers throughout their lifetime, even when they're on their way out the door—even after they've left. You might be surprised by how many ways you can leverage customer relationships to boost retention, obtain referrals, and generate positive reviews.

Don't be afraid to spend more money in this area. It's never a bad idea to invest in retention, and if you have to tighten the belt, tighten it in other areas. Retention is absolutely one of the most important growth levers of your organization, no matter your industry, so it's going to be vitally important for any small business. At the same time, you have to ensure that you've selected the right stakeholders, because they're the ones who are going to help you boost retention.

Beyond customer relationships, thought leadership, partnerships, and solution-selling, there's one other way you can grow your small business, and it might surprise you.

Exercises to Build Your Playbook

- How are you working hard to maintain the post-sale relationship and keep the conversation going?

  _____

  _____

  _____

- Create a calendar for near- and long-term post-sale touches with customers that includes QBRs, surveys, celebratory dinners, special events, follow-up calls, or other forms of regular contact.

- Make a list of three to five customers who would welcome co-publishing white papers, infographics, or articles with you, and jot down some thoughts about what you'd like to co-publish with each of them. Then reach out to them to kick-start the process.

  _____

  _____

  _____

- In what ways can you continue being radically generous to customers even when they leave you (and after they've left)?

_____

_____

_____

11

Creative
Acquisitions

*"The ideology of capitalism makes us all into connoisseurs
of liberty—of the indefinite expansion of possibility."*
—SUSAN SONTAG

I F YOU'RE A VERY SMALL COMPANY, YOU PROBABLY
don't think about acquisitions often, because you assume
they're beyond your ability. So I'll let you in on a little secret:
judicious acquisitions are one of the best ways for a small company
to grow, and they are entirely within your capability.

Most small business leaders don't have a lot of experience with
acquisitions, so they assume you need a ton of money in order to

buy another company. Sometimes, it's possible to borrow earmarked funds for the sole purpose of buying another company, but that's not the only way to do it.

Before we examine those alternatives, let's address a question you might have: why should a small company pursue an acquisition in the first place? As it turns out, there are a lot of reasons. One of the mindset principles we talked about was staying ahead of customer needs, and acquiring another company is one of the fastest and cheapest ways to meet a future customer need, whether that is a geographic location or a technical or practical capability.

Does that sound a little crazy? "We need to meet a customer need, so let's buy a whole company to meet it." At first blush, it might, but the fact is, building a new solution can also be highly expensive *and* take a lot of time, costing you valuable time to market. Acquisition generally takes a lot less time, and while there's still a cost, it can be paid for in a more palatable way. Moreover, depending upon what kind of acquisition you make, it can also come with its own revenue stream.

How can an acquisition allow you to stay ahead of customer needs? In a variety of potential ways. Let's suppose you're a technology company that lacks an entire functionality, but there's another company that has already developed 80 or 90 percent of that functionality. Maybe it's all they do. By acquiring that company, you can integrate their functionality and then either keep or let go of the rest of the company.

Remember, you don't have to keep the entire company. You can buy a piece of it, or you can acquire just its assets. As an example, maybe you're only buying their technology and customers. That way you get the assets without all of the liability, losses, or other problems. In other words, you're taking what you need, not what you don't need or want.

Let's suppose you're losing some customers because you don't have a location they feel they need. Rather than building that location from scratch, you can acquire an existing company there and have something within six to eight weeks that might take you half a year and a lot of money to build on your own. Suddenly, you're competitive in a way you weren't before, getting ahead of a customer need much faster while acquiring a revenue stream, as well.

As we said, retention is one of the most important growth levers, especially for a small company, so anything you can reasonably do to prevent customers from jumping ship in order to meet a need is worth the investment. This is true of prospects, as well. Why would a prospective customer get started with you when they know you might not be able to grow with them? Maybe they don't currently need the Midwest, but they might hope to grow into the region within the next year.

"These people can meet our needs today," they'll think, "but they probably won't meet our needs next year. If we sign with them now, we'll be looking for another company when we get ready to expand into the Midwest. Do we really want to do that?"

DEAL STRUCTURES

How can a still-small company acquire another company? As I said, there are a lot of ways to do it, even when you don't have a lot of cash. There are many different types of deal structures you can come up with. For example, a company might have an asset you need; in turn, their founder might be looking for a vanity exit. A vanity exit is one which allows the owners to advertise that they have been acquired "for an undisclosed sum" so that, even if it wasn't a lot, they can feel good about the announcement.

For instance, maybe the founder isn't doing well, so they're seeking to hand off their company to someone else in a way that will allow them to step aside with dignity. Maybe they've built something nice, but they're just not cut out for business leadership and want to move on or retire. Or perhaps the company is actually distressed.

So, you acquire them and get what you need, and the founder gets a nice press release that says something like, "Acme has been acquired for an undisclosed sum." The founder gets to save face and move forward with their professional life. Everybody wins.

You do have to think about the valuation of a company you want to acquire, but even when a dollar amount has been set, it doesn't mean you have to pay it the minute you take possession. You can pay in tranches (a.k.a. chunks) over time, and you can even connect those tranches to various deliverables. Perhaps the tranche payments are attached to some event that will happen in the future, or they have predetermined times or milestones that trigger them.

For example, the company being acquired might have certain things they say are going to happen, such as financial or product development milestones that directly impact the value of the company. In another structure, some or all of the payment can be attached to a percentage of revenue. Essentially, you can acquire a company in exchange for royalty payments over a certain number of years—and, in that case, no up-front or additional funds are required at all outside of legal fees.

All of these structures are sustainable even for a company that has to operate very leanly. Some of them do not require using, raising, or borrowing any money. No matter how small you are, keep your mind open to the possibility of growth by acquisition; and if the right opportunity presents itself, be fearless but wise. Make sure the conditions exist to elevate and accelerate your company through the acquisition. You don't need millions of dollars parked in an account in order to do this, and you don't have to borrow a huge amount of money that you'll struggle to pay back.

You will have to keep your eyes and ears open in your industry at all times so you can identify a company that is ripe for acquisition as soon as it comes along. Maybe there's a founder who seems to be drawing close to retirement and might be willing to accept an acquisition based on royalty payments for tax purposes. A founder looking for a good way out is probably going to be more amenable to creative acquisition structures. Don't be afraid to reach out and ask.

DUE DILIGENCE

Just beware of a few realities of acquisitions. First, you can't avoid legal fees, and you don't want to skimp on good legal representation. Find the best representation from an attorney who specializes in mergers and acquisitions and be prepared to conduct due diligence. The old saying "caveat emptor" applies: let the buyer beware. Ask about everything so you know exactly what you're getting into before you sign on the dotted line. Make sure you are fully comfortable. Ask all of your questions without hesitation. The prospective acquisition partner might not answer all of them, but you can ask—and pay as much attention to what they *do not say* as to what they do say.

Once you've signed, the company is yours, and everything you didn't ask about is going to come to the surface. It'll be too late then, so create a thorough due diligence list beforehand and make sure you know what you're potentially getting into. One way you can protect yourself is to set aside some funds in escrow against certain specific types of things you may discover post-acquisition during the first year or so. If all is well a year later, then the last bit of money can be released.

Once you acquire a company, you have to successfully integrate it into your company, which is almost always an enormous task. You're integrating their customers and team members as well as their products and services. If they have machinery or technology, you have to integrate that, as well. Part of this process entails figuring out exactly who and what you want to keep, and there are laws about how you conduct group or mass layoffs (and whether you *can* conduct them). Inform your legal counsel so they can clarify any limitations. There might be a required warning period, or filings, or a limited percentage of people who can be let go.

Even if you didn't acquire a company specifically for its people, you have still technically hired them. Don't forget about our mindset principle on hiring the right stakeholders. Consider keeping the people who seem like they can embrace the right mindset going forward, even if you know some training will be necessary.

All of this might sound like a big hassle, but I can say from experience that it's well worth the effort. The legal fees, due diligence, and integration are all worth it in the end—as long as you've acquired the right company. Fortunately, once you've done one or two acquisitions, you'll be a lot better at it. You'll start to understand exactly what to look for, and you will be able to identify the best opportunities quicker and easier.

Don't let the learning curve dissuade you. Think about it—your company could grow by 30 percent overnight just through a single acquisition. I've found that acquisitions are one of the most dramatic ways to achieve *speed to market*, and that's exactly what we're going to talk about next.

Exercises to Build Your Playbook

- What gaps do you have that would be expensive and/or lengthy to fill organically on your own?

  _____

  _____

  _____

- Are there companies you could acquire that would fill in gaps in meeting customer product or service needs?

  _____

  _____

  _____

- Are there companies in geographic markets where you currently lack a presence that you might be able to acquire?

  _____

  _____

  _____

- Make a list of prospective acquisition targets. For each one, list what they would give you as well as what you know of their current status and financial conditions (revenue, debt, etc.).

  _____

  _____

  _____

- Given your current financial situation, what kinds of deal structures would you be able to explore with prospective acquisition targets?

  _____

  _____

  _____

12

Speed to Market

"Life is like a ten-speed bicycle.
Most of us have gears we never use."
—**CHARLES M. SCHULTZ**

THERE'S A CLOCK, AND IT'S TICKING DOWN FAST.
As a small business leader, you can't see it, but it's there all
the time. When it reaches zero, your time will be up. You'll
be out of money, or you'll be beaten by your competitors, and your
opportunity to survive as a company will be gone.

The stark reality for most small businesses is that they have a
fairly small window of time in which to grow if they want to avoid
becoming another statistic out of the many, many small businesses
that fail every year. Beyond merely surviving, there's the possibility

of capturing a market early by moving faster than your competition. This would give you an enormous advantage and allow you to surround yourself with some high barriers to entry as others struggle to catch up.

There's a lot to be said about moving fast and early. Indeed, it's one of the winning tactics of that old childhood game "Bigger and Better." Get in there with your red paperclip and start making smart trades as fast as you can before the hour is up. That's how I walked out of the shopping mall that day long ago with my pink BMX bicycle.

There's an art and a science to creating an enormous amount of value very quickly, so in this final chapter, we're going to take a look at a few key tactics that will contribute to your speed as a small business.

THE POWER OF PARLAYING

A large contributor to speed is something called "parlaying." The term comes from gambling, where it refers to taking your winnings from a previous bet and immediately trying to turn them into an even bigger amount of money with another bet.

In a business context, it means taking something you're doing now and immediately using it as a stepping stone to move your company forward farther and faster. This hearkens back to many of the tactics we've already discussed. For example, we talked quite a bit about positioning yourself as a thought leader in the center of your industry. You don't have to wait for someone else to make you an authority. You can immediately identify yourself as an authority by creating and publishing thought leadership content on your various channels.

In other words, some industry expert doesn't have to give you the title "thought leader." You can just start acting like one. Don't try to wedge your way toward the center of your industry a little at a time, as if you're pushing and shoving your way through a crowd. Position yourself there *immediately* by simply framing your company and what you do through a lens that *places* you in the center. In this context, parlaying means looking at everything you do in terms of how far forward it can catapult your company right now, and then taking that next action immediately.

At all times, ask yourself, "What things can I leverage right now to move my company forward?" Look at absolutely everything you're doing from that perspective. When you interact with a prospect, what next action can you take to move them forward in their relationship with your company? With an existing customer, consider what's going on in their world that you can contribute to.

The same goes for your partner companies. How can you leverage those partnerships right now to move your company forward? It might involve making an audacious request.

"Hey, I noticed you have a blog. Would you be interested in writing for us? Would you let me write for you? Hey, I see you're involved in a trade association. I would love to help with that. Would you be interested in being on one of our advisory councils?"

This is an example of what parlaying looks like. You don't have to create slow processes or take a long time to make progress. In any area of your business, with anything you're doing, don't be afraid to take the next step right away. You might be able to get more accomplished through a single interaction with a prospect, customer, or partner than you realize, just by taking the next action immediately.

Position yourself *now*. Create thought leadership content *now*. Leverage customer and partner relationships *now*. Don't be afraid to ferociously barrel forward. Look right now at how much value you can harvest from every single thing you're doing, and then consider how quickly you can take the next action to move it forward.

This really is like the small business equivalent of kids running around the shopping mall with their little red paperclip, making smart trades as fast as they can in order to create more and more and more value. If you're working on a regional opportunity, find out if it's also a national opportunity. If it's a national opportunity, see if it's also an international one.

If you're working with a customer in one area, see if you can work with them in other areas. Outside of the little bubble of a single opportunity, there's a very large world of other opportunities that can be explored. Beyond the current deal, are there other things that you and a customer could be doing together? Can your current partners introduce you to other companies? What kind of thought leadership could you be doing with your partners that you're not already doing?

They say that running is actually just controlled falling. The fastest runners tend to use running techniques that allow them to run faster while spending less energy. Every step is essentially the runner falling forward, using their own weight to create momentum, and getting ahead of their own feet. That's how it should feel when you're parlaying in business. You're always slightly ahead of your own feet, constantly falling forward at an almost reckless speed.

Whatever you're doing, whatever you're going through, constantly look, ask, and explore what your next step could be for moving your company forward faster and farther. You don't wait for others to create the opportunities for you, and you don't wait until things are perfect. Indeed, *perfect* is the enemy of *good*.

Barrel forward, looking around every single corner to see what's possible. Plant your flag everywhere as quickly as you can. Think really big and act that way. Instead of spending most of your time pondering, planning, and strategizing, adopt a tactical approach of acting on every big opportunity you see in order to extract value from it quickly.

Sometimes, this happens indirectly. For example, if you have a customer or prospect who has a need you can't solve, maybe you can point them to a partner who does. In that way, you're creating value in a partnership through a referral that you can quickly leverage in many ways.

We can reduce this to a simple, clear formula:

Parlaying successfully = thinking big + acting quickly

All of the mindset principles and tactics we've talked about in this book flow right into this tactic. Whether it's being non-transactional, putting yourself at the center of your industry, practicing radical generosity, being disciplined, becoming a thought leader, or anything else, you can barrel forward, moving fast, creating opportunities, and taking the next action right now.

Some people might balk at this recommendation. They'll say, "Big, strategic thinking and speed don't mix well. You can't barrel forward smartly." They assume that deep strategy is a trade-off with speed—you can have one or the other, but not both.

To be clear, sometimes waiting for the right time to do something is absolutely the best approach; but most of the time, being proactive and propelling yourself into the mix is the most advantageous thing you can do. Take new information and act on it right away. Leverage a customer or partner relationship right now. This *is* strategic. You're still being disciplined in everything you do, but you're acting on opportunities with deliberate speed in the broadest way that you can, without putting artificial caps on what you can accomplish at this moment in time.

You have more opportunity to do this when you're a small company—because the bigger you get, the heavier you become, and the more process-oriented you become, with decisions made by committee. Big companies move slower, but as a small company, you can move quickly and start grabbing all of the opportunities that are before you. There are some things you can act on right away that are obvious, and others you're going to have to figure out ways to act on.

It's as simple as looking at everything you're doing right now and finding the next action you can take to move forward. Take every single mindset principle and tactic we've talked about in this book and barrel forward with them. Don't wait for opportunity—*create* opportunity, then reap the rewards.

Exercises to Build Your Playbook

- What things can you do to leverage existing partnerships and customer relationships right now to move your company forward?

  _____

  _____

  _____

- How can you begin acting like a thought leader at the center of your industry right now?

  _____

  _____

  _____

- What next action can you take with prospects to move them forward in their relationship with your company right now?

  _____

  _____

  _____

- What next action can you take to practice radical generosity today?

  _____

  _____

  _____

- What immediate next action can you take to become more disciplined?

  _____

  _____

  _____

Conclusion

It's easy to cobble together a bunch of theoretical growth tactics and publish them, but the strategy I've shared in the preceding chapters has been battle-tested and proved. This approach can indeed help your small business avoid the death spiral that claims 90 percent of small businesses. It works by making you more cash-stable, giving you higher margin as a company, and allowing you to hang on to more of your equity—all while delivering more value to any investors you might have as you build enterprise value.

Remember, I have personally helped lead with this very strategy and achieved 10x growth within around a three-year period, so I know it works. By combining the right mindset principles with a set of specific tactics, I'm confident that you, too, can achieve impressive results in your small business. You don't have to fail. It isn't inevitable. Your small business can grow into a healthy mid-to-large-sized company.

It begins with a non-transactional mindset that focuses on building relationships with customers long before they become a prospect, and continues being radically generous even after they've walked out the door. Position your company at the very center of your industry. Don't wait for someone else to do this for you. Do it now, today. Redefine what you provide in such a way that you are like the hub of a wheel and the rest of your industry like spokes coming out of that hub.

When it comes to your customers, stay ahead of their needs by listening carefully and staying close to them. Radical generosity and thought leadership are going to help you do that, but you should also be using quarterly business reviews, surveys, events, and customer advisory councils—anything to keep the conversation going. Keep being generous to customers even if they leave you, because a former customer can still produce referrals and references, and they might even come back once you can meet their needs. Remember, you're selling *solutions*, not products and services.

By creating partnerships with other companies in your industry—companies that are adjacent to but not competitive with your company—you can share resources and referrals for mutual benefit. Again, practice radical generosity with these companies, giving them more than they give you at all times. It will come back to you in some capacity. It always does.

Finally, don't assume you're too small to pursue acquisitions. There are some creative ways to acquire other companies, if you're willing, including deal structures that work even if you have little money. Acquisitions can be an enormously effective way to grow your company really fast, whether you keep all of the new company or only some of it.

In all of this, be disciplined, aligning everyone and everything in your business with your strategy, and create speed to market by constantly thinking about your next action. Don't sit and wait for something to happen. Leverage relationships, partnerships, and opportunities right now. Create thought leadership and practice radical generosity right now. You should be barreling forward, not tiptoeing, into the future. All of the tactics in this book can be done on a shoestring, and all of them can be done fast (or, at least, faster than you might think!).

TURN THINGS AROUND TODAY

In our opening story, the summer camp kids were only given one hour to trade a single red paperclip for items of increasing value. Whatever we wound up with at the end of that hour was what we took home with us. I walked out of the mall with a pink BMX bicycle, but a few kids walked out of the mall with almost nothing: a stick of gum, a piece of candy, a nickel. Some still had their paperclips and got back on the bus looking utterly defeated. They just couldn't figure out how to create additional value for themselves in such a limited amount of time.

In a small business, you're on a limited time clock, as well. It might be a few years instead of one hour, but it's counting down. And to put it bluntly, the clock is counting down to your extinction. As we've made clear, most small businesses just don't survive; and the ones that do often have to trade much of their equity to investors to do so.

Hopefully, I've made it clear that there are things you can do very quickly with few resources to begin developing great value. As soon as you finish this book, I encourage you to sit down and think about what these mindset principles and tactics would mean for your company in your specific context.

How could you begin to embody each of them in your industry with your specific customers, prospects, and potential partners? How can you position your company at the center of your industry? How can you begin practicing radical generosity and leveraging customer relationships for referrals and references? What thought leadership content are you going to create and publish on your own channels? Which companies in your industry could you partner with for mutual benefit? Are there any opportunities for creative acquisitions?

Since time is running out (and time is always running out when you're a small business, statistically speaking), it might be helpful to create a thirty-day plan for putting some of these mindset principles into action. I believe that if a struggling small business will begin to implement these tactics, they can turn things around almost on a dime.

Some of these tactics might take time to wrap your head around. Maybe you've never imagined that your small business could be at the center of your entire industry. Maybe you've never considered yourself an authoritative thought leader. It's time to put on the crown and start acting like it. No matter who you are, you have ideas and experiences you can share to help people.

Maybe the thought of approaching other companies to create partnerships is intimidating. To make it manageable, you might select just two or three of the principles or tactics in this book and begin focusing on them in your thirty-day plan. See what impact they have on your growth. Then, you can begin implementing the others. Yes, it's going to take some boldness, but no timid company ever achieved incredible results.

The 10x growth that I saw in my own small business wasn't a fluke. I've seen these same principles and tactics work in other companies, as well. There is a way forward for even very small businesses, a lean approach to incredible growth that can be achieved on a shoestring.

And you can get started today—right now!

Acknowledgments

I am filled with deep gratitude to God; to my beloved husband Larry Prozan, who is my rock and support, and who inspires me daily; and to all those who have inspired and influenced me professionally and spiritually over the years, which are too many to note here.

From a professional standpoint, I want to express gratitude for the inspiration and life learnings I have drawn over the years from Brian Firestone, Daphne Carmeli, and Victor Cohn. My deepest thanks to Rafael Zakinov whose egoless leadership style and humanity, which I had the privilege of being around for a number of years inspires me every day. as well as to Eli Mermelstein and Avrami Mermelstein for the countless life and business lessons they've taught me. I also want to acknowledge the unparalleled mentorships of the late Jerry Kalov and the late John McDonald, giants of the consumer electronics industry from whom I have learned lessons that I carry forward daily.

I've had the privilege to work with some of the best people in the world and would like to acknowledge the inspiration and learnings I have drawn from Matt Carpentieri, Jessica Burgess, Claire Bretzke, Raj Kulkarni, Andy Berschauer, Ronojoy Chakrabarti, Chad Stalker, Curtis Mo, and the late George Mueller, inspiring and pioneering founder of Color Kinetics.

No person is an island, and so from a spiritual and communal standpoint for helping shape the better parts of who I am, I want to thank Rabbi Nosson Gurary, Rabbi Joey Felsen, Rabbi Yitzchok Feldman, and Mrs. Nechama Wolfson. I especially would like to honor the blessed memories of the late Rabbi Jacob J. Hecht and Rebbetzin Chave Hecht. Through their founding of the legendary Camp Emunah, where I first played "Bigger and Better" (sometimes known as the Paperclip Game), they laid the empowering spiritual, moral, and leadership foundations for generations of young girls that made us not only feel, but absolutely know deep down in our bones, we could do absolutely anything.

ABOUT THE AUTHOR

Esther Kestenbaum Prozan is a seasoned CEO, president, and CRO who specializes in high-growth environments. She helps companies increase revenue and expand business both organically and by acquisition. Among her achievements, as president at Ruby Has Fulfillment, she led dramatic revenue growth and helped see the business through its acquisition by Shipmonk in a private-equity-backed deal to form the largest privately held e-commerce fulfillment company. She is a board member, strategic advisor, and was on the Top 100 Women in Supply Chain list by IBM and Supply Chain Digital. She has written in numerous business publications and is a *Forbes*, *Entrepreneur*, and *Fast Company* contributor.